Math in F⊙CUS®

Singapore Math®
by Marshall Cavendish

Extra Practice and Homework

Program Consultant
Dr. Fong Ho Kheong

Author
Sophie Shieh

Grade
KB

Marshall Cavendish
Education

U.S. Distributor

Houghton Mifflin Harcourt.
The Learning Company™

© 2020 Marshall Cavendish Education Pte Ltd

Published by Marshall Cavendish Education
Times Centre, 1 New Industrial Road, Singapore 536196
Customer Service Hotline: (65) 6213 9688
US Office Tel: (1-914) 332 8888 | Fax: (1-914) 332 8882
E-mail: cs@mceducation.com
Website: www.mceducation.com

Distributed by
Houghton Mifflin Harcourt
125 High Street
Boston, MA 02110
Tel: 617-351-5000
Website: www.hmhco.com/programs/math-in-focus

First published 2020

All rights reserved. No part of this publication may be reproduced, stored in a retrieval system or transmitted, in any form or by any means, electronic, mechanical, photocopying, recording or otherwise, without the prior written permission of Marshall Cavendish Education. If you have received these materials as examination copies free of charge, Marshall Cavendish Education retains the rights to the materials and they may not be resold. Resale of examination copies is strictly prohibited.

Marshall Cavendish and *Math in Focus®* are registered trademarks of Times Publishing Limited.

Singapore Math® is a trademark of Singapore Math Inc.® and Marshall Cavendish Education Pte Ltd.

ISBN 978-0-358-10297-7

Printed in Singapore

1 2 3 4 5 6 7 8   1401   25 24 23 22 21 20
4500759430   A B C D E

The cover image shows a lop-eared rabbit.
In the wild, rabbits come out at night to feed on grass.
The low light keeps them safe.
Rabbits like to chew on tough things like twigs, bark, and carrots.
This is because their teeth never stop growing!
They chew to keep their teeth short.

Contents

© 2020 Marshall Cavendish Education Pte Ltd

© 2020 Marshall Cavendish Education Pte Ltd

© 2020 Marshall Cavendish Education Pte Ltd

Preface

Welcome!

This is what you will do in **Math in Focus®** *Extra Practice and Homework*.

- Practice what you learn in **Activities**.

- Share your thinking in **MATH JOURNAL**.

- Think hard, as you solve problems in **PUT ON YOUR THINKING CAP!**

Bring home the **SCHOOL-to-HOME CONNECTIONS** letter at the start of each chapter. The letter shows your family what you are learning in school. There are some activities in the letter and your family can do them with you to help you to learn even more!

© 2020 Marshall Cavendish Education Pte Ltd

SCHOOL-to-HOME
CONNECTIONS

Chapter **6**

Numbers to 20

Dear Family,

In this chapter, your child will work with numbers to 20. Skills your child will practice include:

- counting, reading, and writing numbers from 10 to 20
- counting on and counting back from 0 to 20
- order numbers to 20
- taking apart numbers to 20

Math Practice

At the end of this chapter, you may want to carry out these activities with your child. These activities will help to support your child as he or she learns numbers to 20.

Activity 1

- Write the numbers 10 to 20 on separate cards.
- Have your child close his or her eyes as you put the cards down in order, leaving one card in your hand.
- Ask your child to open his or her eyes, say the numbers on the cards from least to greatest, and figure out which number is missing.
- Have your child check the card in your hand to confirm his or her answer. Return the card to the set before your child leads the next round.

Math Talk

Gather 20 identical objects and 2 paper plates. Put 10 objects on the first plate and up to 10 objects on the second plate. Ask your child to **count** the objects on the first plate and then **count on** to find the total number of objects on both plates. Let your child lead the next round.

© 2020 Marshall Cavendish Education Pte Ltd

Activity 2

- Draw two ten frames as shown below.
- Gather 20 identical objects such as fish crackers or dried beans to place on the frames.
- Take turns filling each space in the first ten frame and any number of spaces in the second frame. Count to 10 and then count on to find the total number of objects.
- Empty the frames before your child leads the next round.

Ten Frames

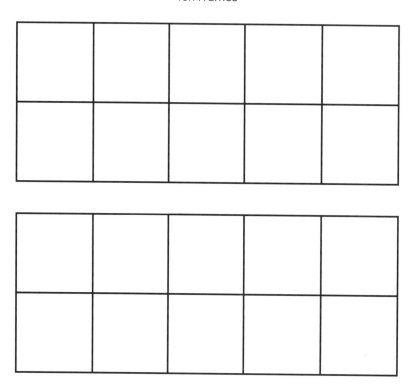

© 2020 Marshall Cavendish Education Pte Ltd

Chapter 6

Extra Practice and Homework
Numbers to 20

Activity 1   Numbers 11 to 13

Count on from 10.
Write each number.

 1

10

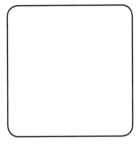

© 2020 Marshall Cavendish Education Pte Ltd

2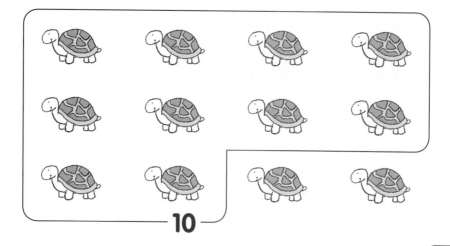

10

3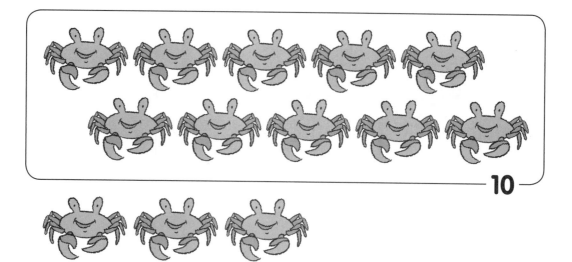

10

© 2020 Marshall Cavendish Education Pte Ltd

Circle to make a 10.
Count on.
Write each number.

© 2020 Marshall Cavendish Education Pte Ltd

Draw to make a 10 in the **.**
Next, draw to count on.
Then, fill in each blank.

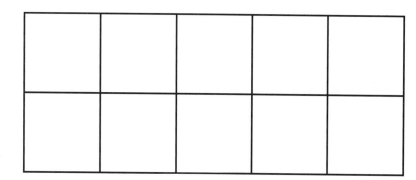

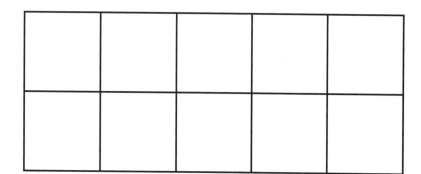

10 and _____ make _____.

© 2020 Marshall Cavendish Education Pte Ltd

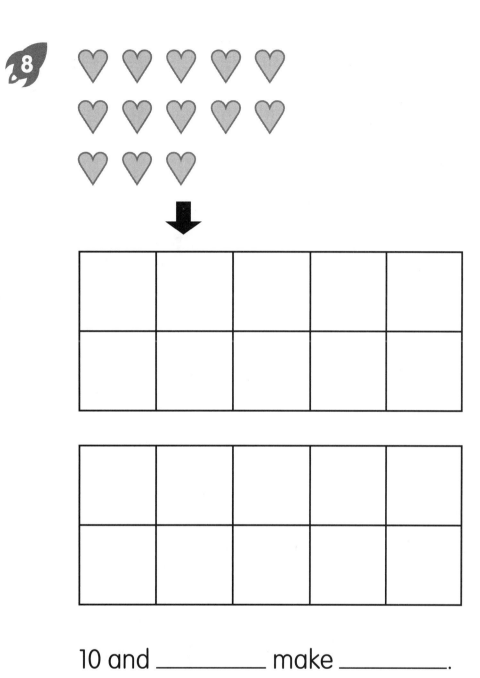

10 and _____ make _____.

© 2020 Marshall Cavendish Education Pte Ltd

Count.
Circle each correct number.

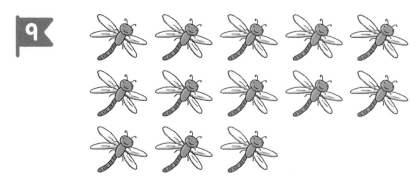

11 **13** **9**

11 **10** **13**

11 **10** **12**

© 2020 Marshall Cavendish Education Pte Ltd

Extra Practice and Homework Grade KB

Color eleven  **blue.**

Color twelve ![] **yellow.**

Color thirteen ![] **red.**

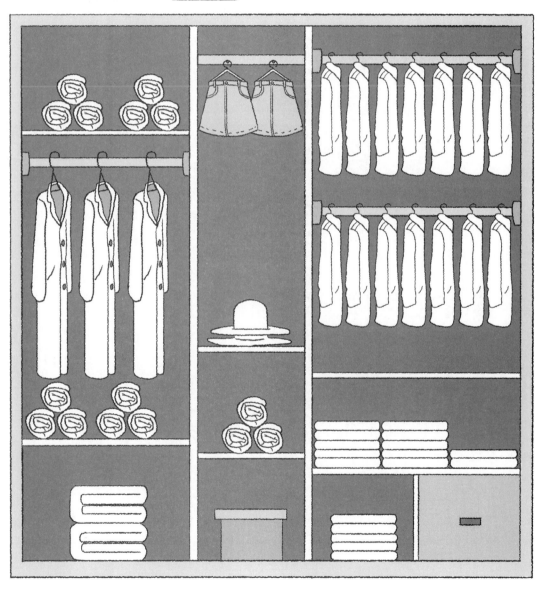

© 2020 Marshall Cavendish Education Pte Ltd

Count.
Match.

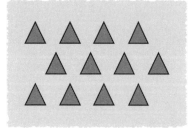

•   • eleven

•   • twelve

•   • thirteen

© 2020 Marshall Cavendish Education Pte Ltd

Chapter 6

Extra Practice and Homework
Numbers to 20

Activity 2   Numbers 14 to 16

Count on from 10.
Write each number.

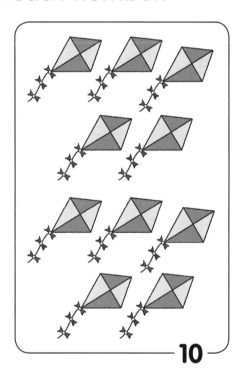

10

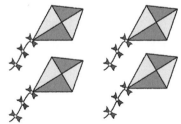

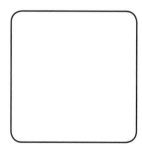

© 2020 Marshall Cavendish Education Pte Ltd

2

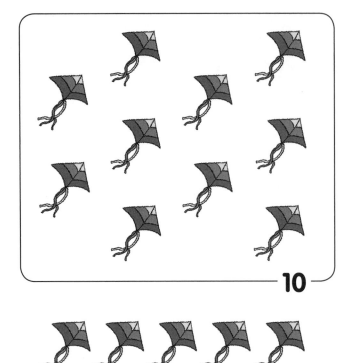

10

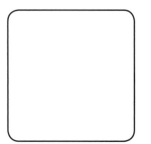

3

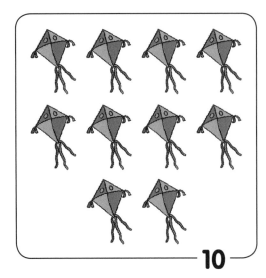

10

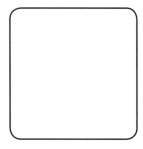

© 2020 Marshall Cavendish Education Pte Ltd

Circle to make a 10.
Count on.
Write each number.

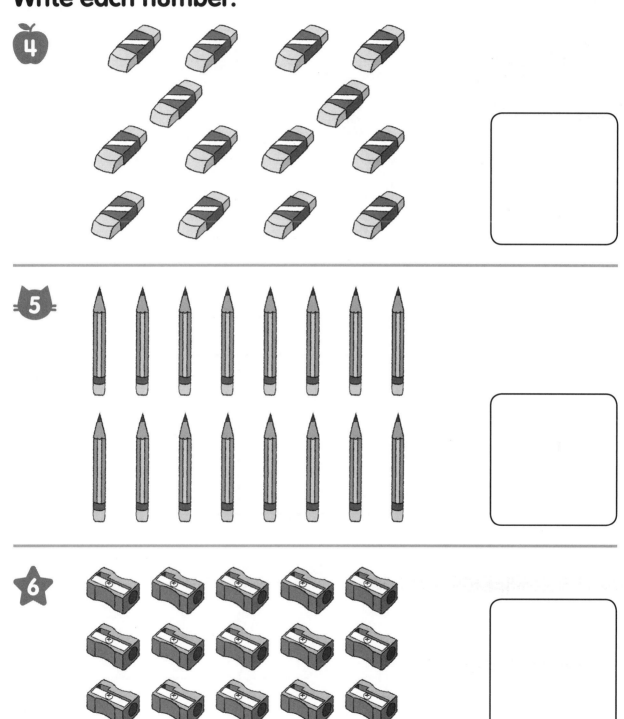

© 2020 Marshall Cavendish Education Pte Ltd

Draw to make a 10 in the  **.**
Next, draw to count on.
Then, fill in each blank.

 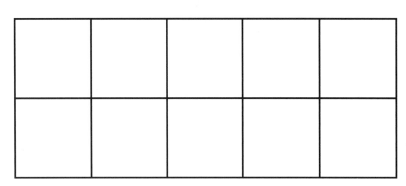

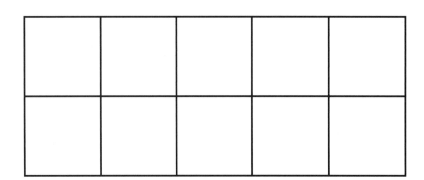

10 and _____ make _____.

Extra Practice and Homework Grade KB

© 2020 Marshall Cavendish Education Pte Ltd

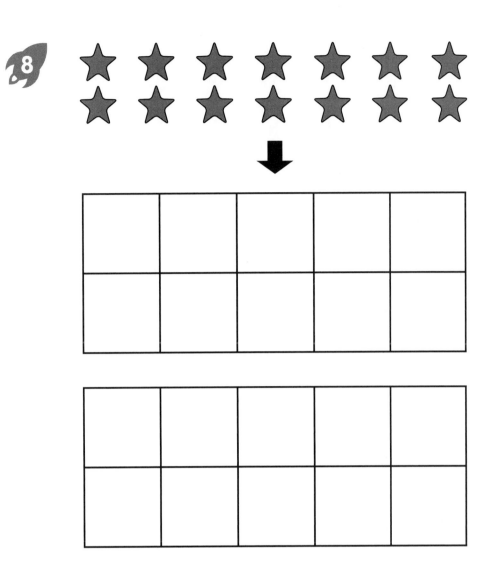

10 and _____ make _____.

© 2020 Marshall Cavendish Education Pte Ltd

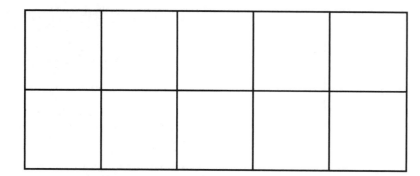

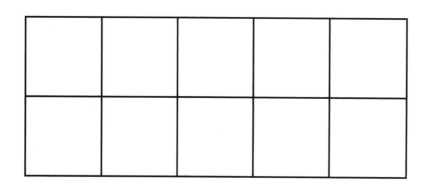

10 and _____ make _____.

© 2020 Marshall Cavendish Education Pte Ltd

Count.
Match.

•

• fourteen

•

• sixteen

•

• fifteen

© 2020 Marshall Cavendish Education Pte Ltd

BLANK

Chapter 6

Extra Practice and Homework
Numbers to 20

Activity 3 Numbers 17 to 20

Count on from 10.
Write each number.

10

© 2020 Marshall Cavendish Education Pte Ltd

2

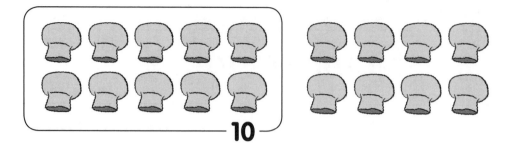

3

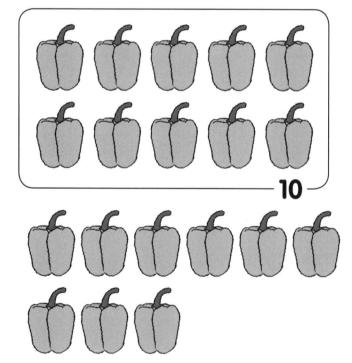

© 2020 Marshall Cavendish Education Pte Ltd

© 2020 Marshall Cavendish Education Pte Ltd

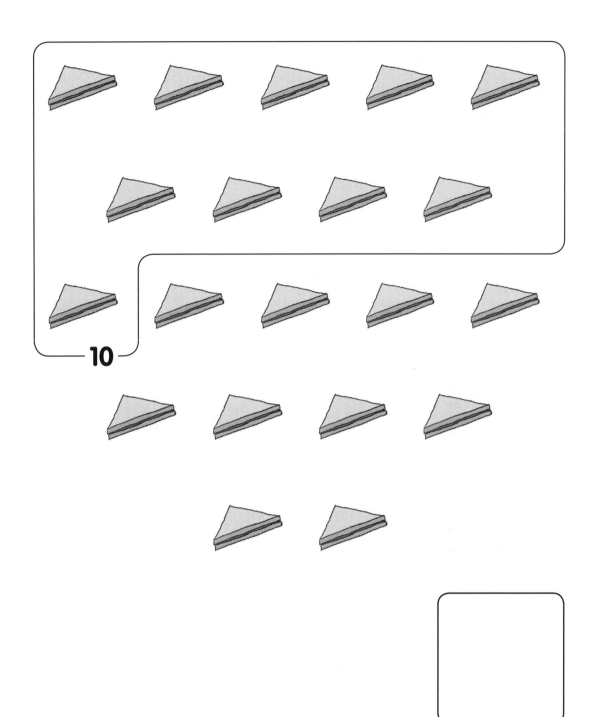

10

3 Numbers 17 to 20 **21**

Circle to make a 10.
Count on.
Write each number.

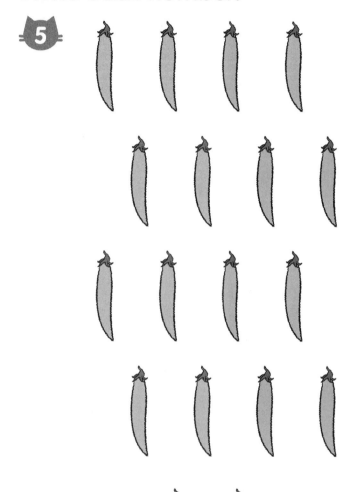

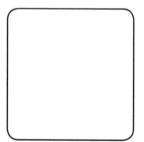

© 2020 Marshall Cavendish Education Pte Ltd

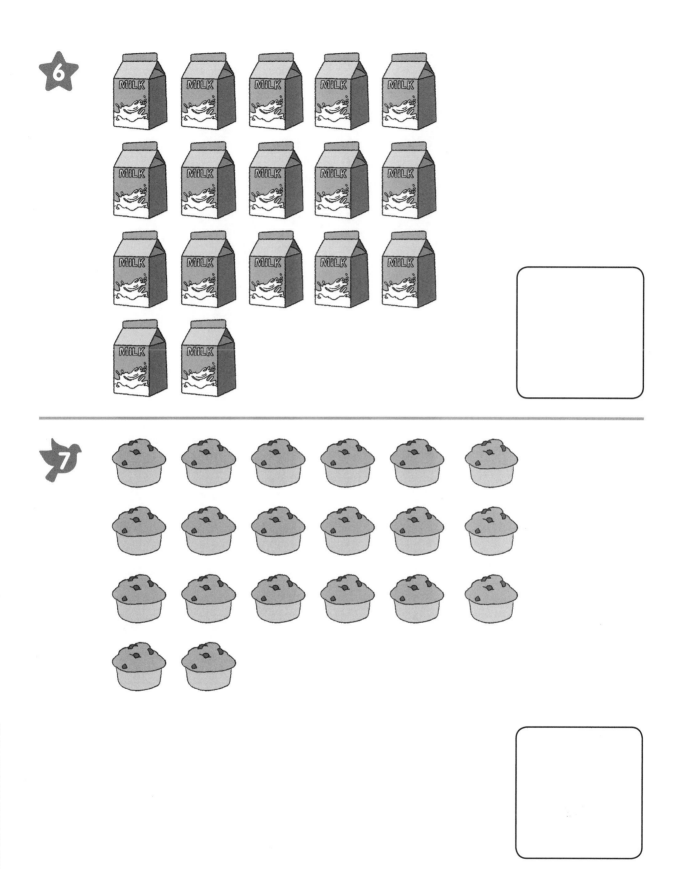

© 2020 Marshall Cavendish Education Pte Ltd

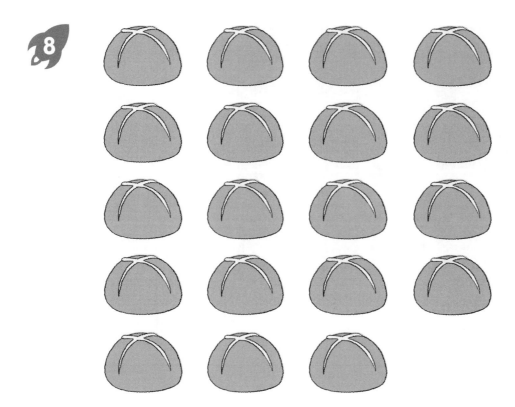

© 2020 Marshall Cavendish Education Pte Ltd

Draw to make a 10 in the ⬚⬚⬚⬚⬚ .
Next, draw to count on.
Then, fill in each blank.

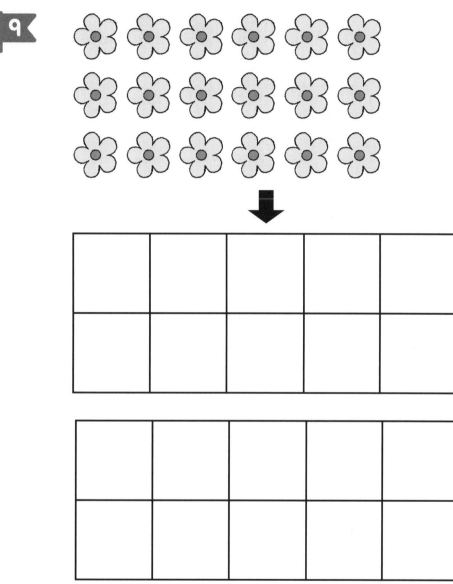

9

10 and _____ make _____.

© 2020 Marshall Cavendish Education Pte Ltd

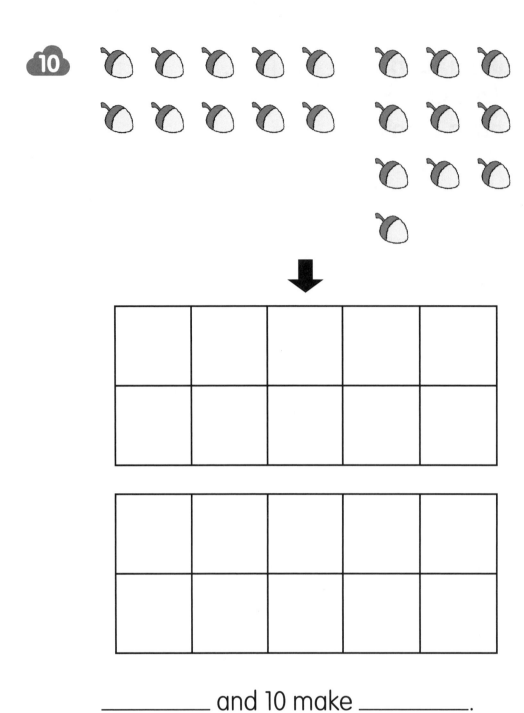

_____ and 10 make _____.

© 2020 Marshall Cavendish Education Pte Ltd

Count.
Match.

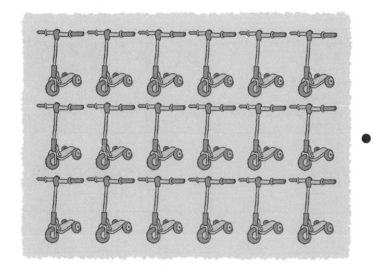

© 2020 Marshall Cavendish Education Pte Ltd

Count.
Circle each correct number word.

| twenty | seventeen |

| nineteen | eighteen |

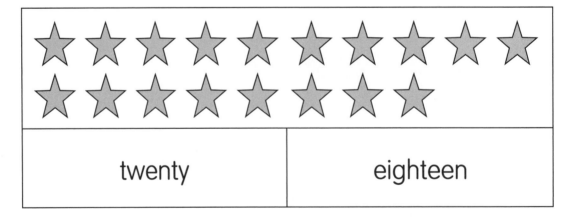

| twenty | eighteen |

Extra Practice and Homework Grade KB

© 2020 Marshall Cavendish Education Pte Ltd

Chapter 6

Extra Practice and Homework
Numbers to 20

Activity 4   Order Numbers to 20

Count on.
Write each missing number.

11 | | | 14 | 15

14 | | | 17 | 18

© 2020 Marshall Cavendish Education Pte Ltd

© 2020 Marshall Cavendish Education Pte Ltd

Count back.
Write each missing number.

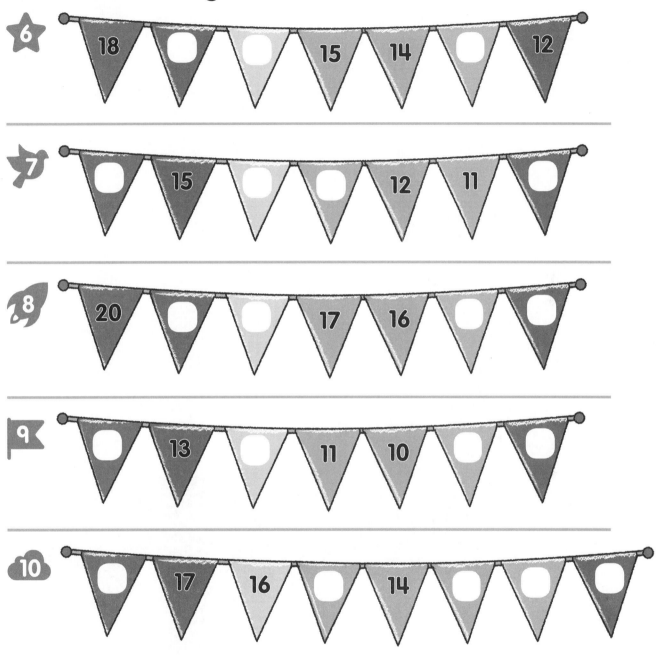

6 18 ◯ ◯ 15 14 ◯ 12

7 ◯ 15 ◯ ◯ 12 11 ◯

8 20 ◯ ◯ 17 16 ◯ ◯

9 ◯ 13 ◯ 11 10 ◯ ◯

10 ◯ 17 16 ◯ 14 ◯ ◯ ◯

© 2020 Marshall Cavendish Education Pte Ltd

Count on from 10.
Write each missing number.

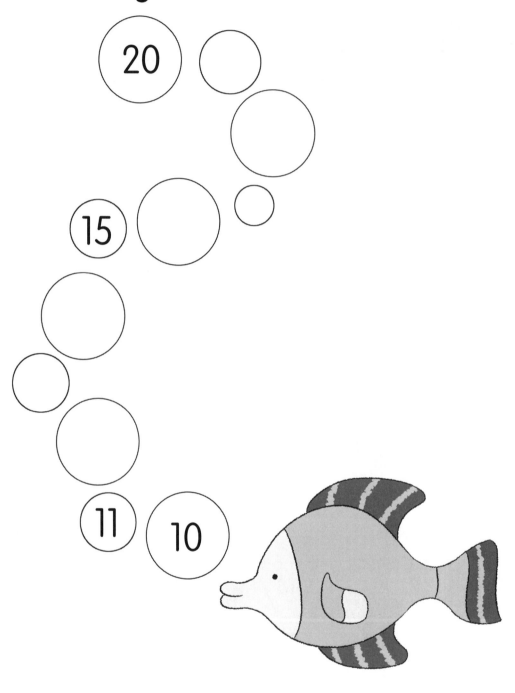

© 2020 Marshall Cavendish Education Pte Ltd

Chapter 6 Extra Practice and Homework
Numbers to 20

Activity 5   Take Apart Numbers to 20

Circle to make a 10.
Fill in each blank.

 There are 12 .

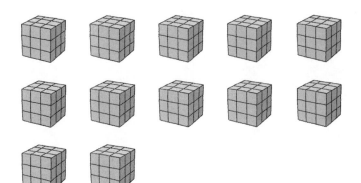

12 is _____ and _____.

---

2 There are 13 English.

13 is _____ and _____.

© 2020 Marshall Cavendish Education Pte Ltd

3 There are 15 .

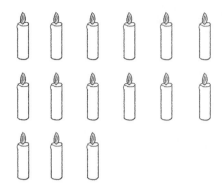

15 is _____ and _____.

---

4 There are 18 .

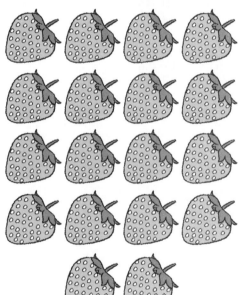

18 is _____ and _____.

© 2020 Marshall Cavendish Education Pte Ltd

5 There are 17 .

17 is _____ and _____.

 6

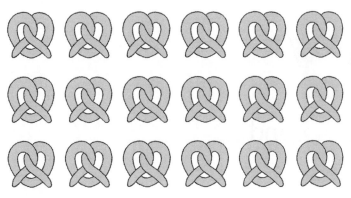

19 is _____ and _____.

© 2020 Marshall Cavendish Education Pte Ltd

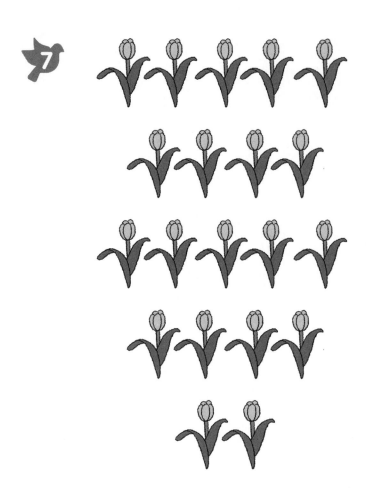

20 is _____ and _____.

© 2020 Marshall Cavendish Education Pte Ltd

Count.
Fill in each blank.

  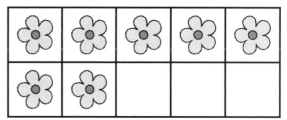

14 is _____ and _____.

10 and _____ make _____.

 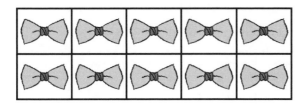 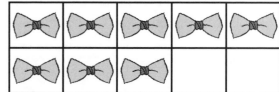

10 and _____ make _____.

_____ is 10 and _____.

© 2020 Marshall Cavendish Education Pte Ltd

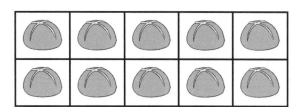 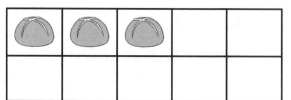

10 and _____ make _____.

_____ is 10 and _____.

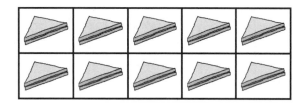 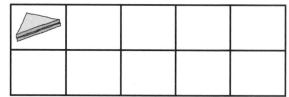

_____ and _____ make _____.

_____ is _____ and _____.

 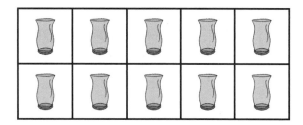 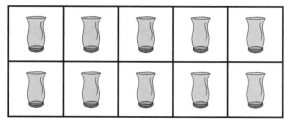

_____ and _____ make _____.

_____ is _____ and _____.

© 2020 Marshall Cavendish Education Pte Ltd

MATH JOURNAL

 Mathematical Habit 2 Use mathematical reasoning

1 David has a party.

He bakes 12 .

He makes 14 .

He buys 16 .

Draw the party food below.

© 2020 Marshall Cavendish Education Pte Ltd

Mathematical Habit 2 **Use mathematical reasoning**

2 Jade has 20 color pencils.

Some of her color pencils are here.

Draw the rest of the color pencils.

Extra Practice and Homework Grade KB

© 2020 Marshall Cavendish Education Pte Ltd

Mathematical Habit 1 **Persevere in solving problems**

 Molly and John share some beads.

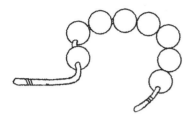 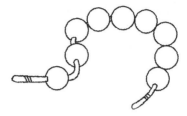

Molly   John

a Molly has _____ beads.

John has _____ beads.

b Fill in each blank from **a**.

_____ and _____ is the same as

10 and _____.

10 and _____ make _____.

_____ is _____ and _____.

© 2020 Marshall Cavendish Education Pte Ltd

PUT ON YOUR THINKING CAP!

Mathematical Habit **1** **Persevere in solving problems**

2 Show another way they can share the beads.

a Draw the beads in each box.

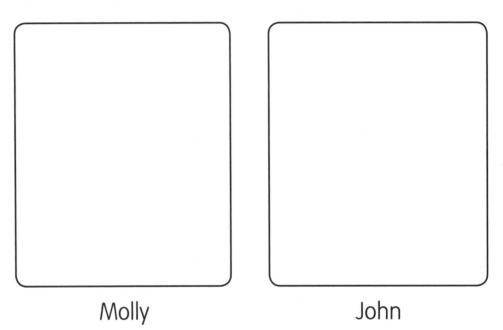

Molly   John

b Fill in each blank.

_____ and _____ make _____.

_____ is _____ and _____.

© 2020 Marshall Cavendish Education Pte Ltd

SCHOOL-to-HOME
CONNECTIONS

Chapter 7 Addition

Dear Family,

In this chapter, your child will learn about addition. Skills your child will practice include:
- adding by putting together and adding to
- using addition facts to 5 to add
- counting on to add numbers to 10
- writing and solving addition sentences

Math Activities

At the end of this chapter, you may want to carry out these activities with your child. These activities will help to support your child as he or she adds within 10.

Activity 1

- Gather dominoes with number parts that add to 10 or less or go online to print free printable dominoes as shown below and cut them out.
- Put the dominoes in a paper bag.
- Pick a domino, count the dots, and add to find the sum.
- Return the domino to the bag before your child leads the next round.

 Math Talk

Gather 10 identical objects and a number cube. Take 1 to 4 objects and count aloud. Roll the number cube and take the corresponding number of objects. Ask your child to count on to add. Encourage your child to use the words **put together** and **add to**. Return objects before the next round.

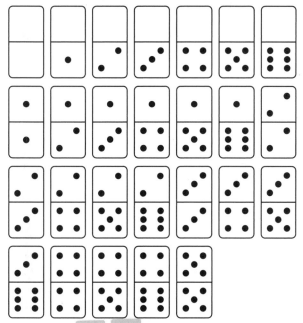

© 2020 Marshall Cavendish Education Pte Ltd

BLANK

Chapter 7

Extra Practice and Homework
Addition

Activity 1　Addition Stories

Use each picture to make an addition story.
Fill in each blank.

Adam builds 3 .

Sarah builds _____ .

Adam and Sarah build _____ in all.

© 2020 Marshall Cavendish Education Pte Ltd

_____  are on the ground.

_____ join them.

There are _____ in all.

© 2020 Marshall Cavendish Education Pte Ltd

3

Lucy

Lucy has _____  .

Lucy gets _____  more.

Lucy has _____  in all.

© 2020 Marshall Cavendish Education Pte Ltd

There are _____  in the 🏺 .

Jane puts _____ 🌷 more in the 🏺 .

There are _____ 🌷 in all.

© 2020 Marshall Cavendish Education Pte Ltd

5

_____  are in the 🧺.

_____  are **not** in the 🧺.

There are _____  in all.

© 2020 Marshall Cavendish Education Pte Ltd

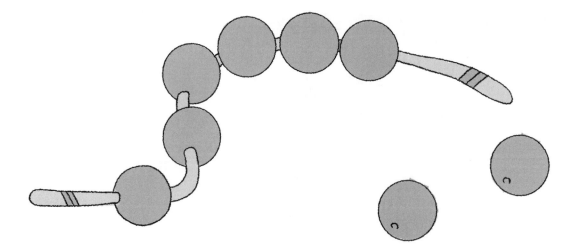

June has _____ ⚬ in a 〰.

She has _____ more ⚬.

June has _____ ⚬ in all.

© 2020 Marshall Cavendish Education Pte Ltd

Draw 7 .
Fill in each blank.

7 Draw some in the box.

Draw the rest of the outside the box.

_____ are in the box.

_____ are **not** in the box.

There are _____ in all.

© 2020 Marshall Cavendish Education Pte Ltd

Color 6 .
Fill in each blank.

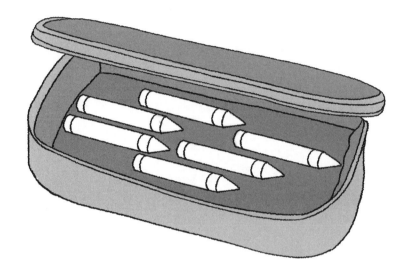

Color some ✏ red.

Color the rest of the ✏ blue.

_____ ✏ are red.

_____ ✏ are blue.

There are _____ ✏ in all.

© 2020 Marshall Cavendish Education Pte Ltd

2 How many are there in all?

3

2

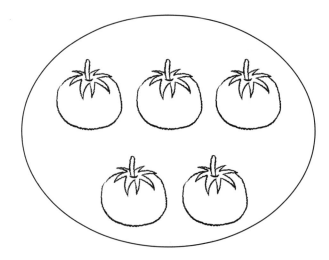

3 and 2 make _____.

There are _____ in all.

© 2020 Marshall Cavendish Education Pte Ltd

Chapter 7

Extra Practice and Homewo
Addition

Activity 2   Put Together and Add To

Fill in each blank.

 How many  are there in all?

2   1

2 and 1 make _____.

There are _____ in all.

© 2020 Marshall Cavendish Education Pte Ltd

Draw.
Fill in each blank.

 How many are there in all?

1

3

1 and 3 make _____.

There are _____ in all.

© 2020 Marshall Cavendish Education Pte Ltd

4 How many are there in all?

2   2

2 and 2 make _____.

There are _____ ⭐ in all.

© 2020 Marshall Cavendish Education Pte Ltd

Fill in each blank.

 5 How many ladybugs are there in all?

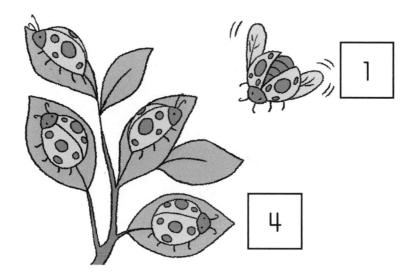

_____ and _____ make _____.

There are _____ ladybugs in all.

---

 6 How many rabbits are there in all?

_____ and _____ make _____.

There are _____ rabbits in all.

© 2020 Marshall Cavendish Education Pte Ltd

How many frogs are there in all?

a

3

1

_____ and _____ make _____.

There are _____ frogs in all.

b

4

0

_____ and _____ make _____.

There are _____ frogs in all.

 © 2020 Marshall Cavendish Education Pte Ltd

Chapter 7

Extra Practice and Homework
Addition

Activity 3   Add Fluently Within 5

How many are there in all?
Fill in each blank.

1 and 2 is the same as _____.

1 + 2 = _____

2 and 1 is the same as _____.

_____ + _____ = _____

There are _____ leaves in all.

© 2020 Marshall Cavendish Education Pte Ltd

2

_____ + _____ = _____ or

_____ + _____ = _____.

There are _____ mice in all.

3

3 + 2 = _____ or

2 + 3 = _____

There are _____ party hats in all.

© 2020 Marshall Cavendish Education Pte Ltd

4

_____ + _____ = _____ or

_____ + _____ = _____

There are _____ toys in all.

 5

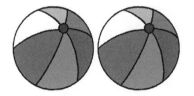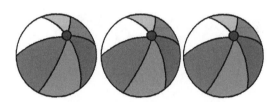

_____ + _____ = _____ or

_____ + _____ = _____

There are _____ balls in all.

© 2020 Marshall Cavendish Education Pte Ltd

Add.

 6

3   +   2   = _____

 7

_____   +   1   =   3

 8

1   +   _____   = _____

© 2020 Marshall Cavendish Education Pte Ltd

Add.

1 + 2 = _____

_____ + 1 = _____

---

2 + _____ = _____

© 2020 Marshall Cavendish Education Pte Ltd

Fill in each blank.

 12 3 + 1 = _____

 13 3 + 2 = _____

 14 1 + 4 = _____

15 3 + 0 = _____

Draw 5 △.

Then, fill in each blank.

 16 Color some △ green.

Color the rest orange.

_____ ◯ _____ ◯ 5

© 2020 Marshall Cavendish Education Pte Ltd

Chapter 7 Extra Practice and Homework
Addition

Activity 4   Add Within 10

How many are there in all?
Fill in each blank.

5 + 1 = _____

There are _____ flowers in all.

© 2020 Marshall Cavendish Education Pte Ltd

How many eggs are there in all?
Draw to show the story.
Fill in each blank.

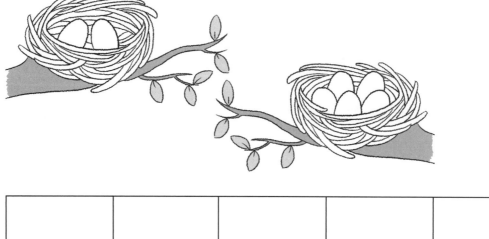

<table>
<tr><td></td><td></td><td></td><td></td><td></td></tr>
<tr><td></td><td></td><td></td><td></td><td></td></tr>
</table>

2 + _____ = _____

There are _____ eggs in all.

© 2020 Marshall Cavendish Education Pte Ltd

How many are there in all?
Count on to add.
Fill in each blank.

3

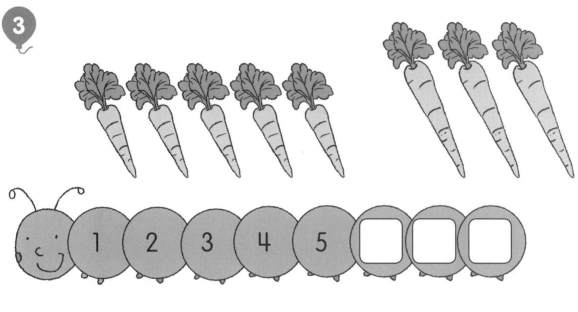

$5 + 3 =$ _____

There are _____ carrots in all.

4

$2 + 7 =$ _____

There are _____ dinosaurs in all.

© 2020 Marshall Cavendish Education Pte Ltd

Count to add.
Fill in each blank.

5 6 + 2 = _____

6 5 + 4 = _____

7 4 + 4 = _____

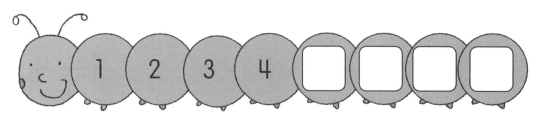

8 7 + 3 = _____

© 2020 Marshall Cavendish Education Pte Ltd

Chapter 7

Extra Practice and Homework
Addition

Activity 5   Addition Sentences

Solve.
Fill in each blank.

 1 4 children are in the boats.
1 boy is getting into the boat.
How many children are there in all?

4 + _____ = _____

There are _____ children in all.

© 2020 Marshall Cavendish Education Pte Ltd

2 5 bees are on a hive.
4 bees are on another hive.
How many bees are there in all?

5 + _____ = _____

There are _____ bees in all.

One nest has 8 eggs.
The other nest has none.
How many eggs are there in all?

_____ + _____ = _____

There are _____ eggs in all.

© 2020 Marshall Cavendish Education Pte Ltd

4 Jose is at the cashier.
There are 6 people waiting in line behind her.
How many people are there in all?

Jose

_____ + _____ = _____

There are _____ people in all.

---

5 There are 5 ducks in a pond.
There are no ducks on the grass.
How many ducks are there in all?

_____ + _____ = _____

There are _____ ducks in all.

© 2020 Marshall Cavendish Education Pte Ltd

Add.
Fill in each blank.

 Thomas has 3 black T-shirts.
He has 4 gray T-shirts.
How many T-shirts does Thomas have in all?

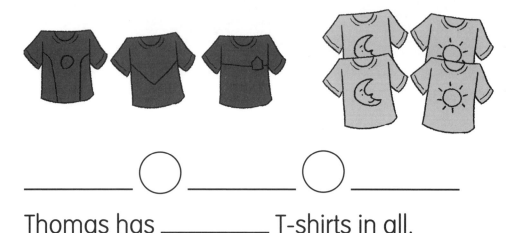

_____ ◯ _____ ◯ _____

Thomas has _____ T-shirts in all.

 There are 4 big ants on a leaf.
There are 4 small ants on the leaf.
How many ants are there on the leaf in all?

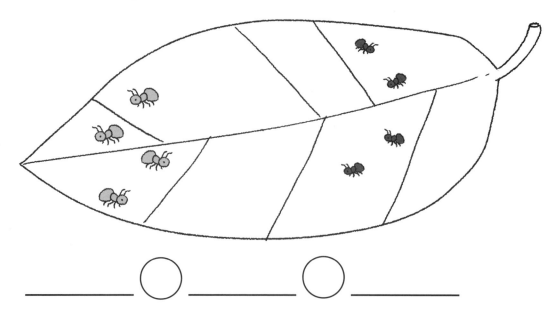

_____ ◯ _____ ◯ _____

There are _____ ants on the leaf in all.

© 2020 Marshall Cavendish Education Pte Ltd

Mathematical Habit 6 Use precise mathematical language

Look at the picture.
Fill in each blank.

a   There are _____ apples on the tree.

There are _____ apples on the ground.

_____ ◯ _____ ◯ _____

There are _____ apples in all.

b   Make another addition story from the picture.
Tell your story to your partner.

© 2020 Marshall Cavendish Education Pte Ltd

PUT ON YOUR THINKING CAP!

1 Mathematical Habit **4** Use mathematical models

Look at the picture.
Make three addition stories.

Write an addition sentence for each story.

Use ⬚ to help you.

_____ ◯ _____ ◯ _____

_____ ◯ _____ ◯ _____

_____ ◯ _____ ◯ _____

© 2020 Marshall Cavendish Education Pte Ltd

Mathematical Habit 1 Persevere in solving problems

a Kim makes 4 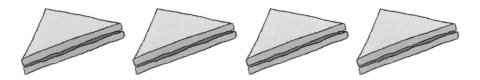.

Jason makes the same number of ◿.

How many ◿ do they have in all?

_____ + _____ = _____

They have _____ ◿ in all.

b They want to make 10 ◿ in all.

How many more ◿ do they have to make?

_____ + _____ = 10

They have to make _____ more ◿.

© 2020 Marshall Cavendish Education Pte Ltd

BLANK

SCHOOL-to-HOME CONNECTIONS

Chapter 8 Subtraction

Dear Family,

In this chapter, your child will learn about subtraction. Skills your child will practice include:
- subtracting by taking from and taking apart
- using subtraction facts to 5 to subtract
- counting back to subtract numbers to 10
- writing and solving subtraction sentences

Math Activities

At the end of this chapter, you may want to carry out these activities with your child. These activities will help to support your child as he or she subtracts within 10.

Activity 1
- Gather 10 paper cups and a small foam or plastic ball.
- Assemble all cups like bowling pins and roll the foam ball to knock them down.
- Call out a subtraction sentence after the roll, such as "10 take away 4 is six."
- Have your child lead the next round.

Activity 2
- Gather 10 identical objects such as dried beans or seashells and a number cube.
- Roll the number cube and take away objects that match the number on the cube.
- Call out a subtraction sentence after the roll such as "10 take away 4 is six."
- Have your child lead the next round.

Activity 3
- Gather 10 identical objects such as blocks or beads and a paper cup.
- Scatter some objects on a flat surface and count them.
- Use the cup to hide some objects that are scattered and ask your child, "How many did I take away?". Give your child time to figure out the answer before revealing the number of objects hidden under the cup.
- Repeat the activity several times.

Math Talk

Gather 10 identical objects. Take 2 to 5 objects and say, "I'm going to take away 2 objects." Remove 2 objects, and have your child count the objects that remain. Ask, "How many objects are left?" Repeat the activity by using and removing a different number of objects.

© 2020 Marshall Cavendish Education Pte Ltd

BLANK

Name: _____ Date: _____

Chapter 8 Extra Practice and Homework
Subtraction

Activity 1   Subtraction Stories

Use the pictures to make a subtraction story.
Fill in each blank.

There are _____ flying over the .

_____ sit on the .

There are _____ left flying over the .

© 2020 Marshall Cavendish Education Pte Ltd

2

There are _____  .

_____  walk away.

There are _____  left.

© 2020 Marshall Cavendish Education Pte Ltd

3

There are _____ in the tree.

_____ 🐒 swing away.

There are _____ 🐒 left in the tree.

© 2020 Marshall Cavendish Education Pte Ltd

There are _____ .

_____  hop away.

There are _____  left.

© 2020 Marshall Cavendish Education Pte Ltd

Jack has _____  .

_____  fly off.

Jack has _____  left.

© 2020 Marshall Cavendish Education Pte Ltd

© 2020 Marshall Cavendish Education Pte Ltd

There are _____ .

_____ are drinking.

_____ are **not** drinking.

There are _____  .

_____  is **not** looking for 🐟 .

There are _____  looking for 🐟 .

© 2020 Marshall Cavendish Education Pte Ltd

There are _____  on the sand.

_____  go in the water.

There are _____  left on the sa

© 2020 Marshall Cavendish Education Pte Ltd

Chapter 8

Extra Practice and Homework
Subtraction

Activity 2   Take From and Take Apart

Fill in each blank.

 1

3 is 1 and _____.

There are _____ .

2

4 is 2 and _____.

There are _____ .

© 2020 Marshall Cavendish Education Pte Ltd

Fill in each blank.

3

There are _____ children in all.

_____ children get down from the .

5 is _____ and _____.

_____ children are left on the .

© 2020 Marshall Cavendish Education Pte Ltd

There are _____ in all.

Ella takes _____ from the ⬭_____.

4 is _____ and _____.

_____ are left on the ⬭_____.

© 2020 Marshall Cavendish Education Pte Ltd

5

There are _____  in all.

Daniel puts _____ on the _____.

_____ is _____ and _____.

There is _____ left.

© 2020 Marshall Cavendish Education Pte Ltd

6

Ms. Lopez buys 5 .

She gives away _____ .

_____ is _____ and _____ .

Now, Ms. Lopez has _____  left.

7

There are _____  in all.

Thomas takes _____ .

_____ is _____ and _____ .

There are _____  left.

© 2020 Marshall Cavendish Education Pte Ltd

BLANK

Chapter 8

Extra Practice and Homework
Subtraction

Activity 3   Subtract Fluently Within 5

Subtract.
Fill in each blank.

3 – 1 = _____ or

3 – 2 = _____

4 – 2 = _____ or

_____ – _____ = _____

© 2020 Marshall Cavendish Education Pte Ltd

3

_____ – _____ = _____ or

_____ – _____ = _____

4

_____ – _____ = _____ or

_____ – _____ = _____

5

_____ – _____ = _____ or

_____ – _____ = _____

© 2020 Marshall Cavendish Education Pte Ltd

_____ – _____ = _____ or

_____ – _____ = _____

_____ – _____ = _____ or

_____ – _____ = _____

_____ – _____ = _____ or

_____ – _____ = _____

© 2020 Marshall Cavendish Education Pte Ltd

Subtract.
Fill in each blank.

9 How many fly away?

5 − 2 = _____

_____  fly away.

© 2020 Marshall Cavendish Education Pte Ltd

10 How many are still in the ?

_____ – _____ = _____

_____ are still in the 🥚.

---

11 How many eggs have **not** hatched?

_____ – _____ = _____

_____ eggs have **not** hatched.

© 2020 Marshall Cavendish Education Pte Ltd

Subtract.
Match each to a .

5 – 3   •

0   •

4 – 3   •

4   •

4 – 4   •

1   •

5 – 1   •

2   •

5 – 2   •

3   •

Extra Practice and Homework Grade KB

© 2020 Marshall Cavendish Education Pte Ltd

Chapter 8 Extra Practice and Homework
Subtraction

Activity 4   Subtract Within 10

Color the ◯ **to show the story.**
Subtract.
Fill in each blank.

How many 🍋 are left on the tree?

7 − 3 = _____

There are _____ 🍋 left on the tree.

© 2020 Marshall Cavendish Education Pte Ltd

2

How many  are left on the flowers?

8 − 6 = _____

There are _____  left on the flowers.

© 2020 Marshall Cavendish Education Pte Ltd

How many are left?

9 − _____ = _____

There are _____ 🥤 left.

© 2020 Marshall Cavendish Education Pte Ltd

4

How many good are left?

6 – _____ = _____

There are _____ good left.

Draw and color some ◯ **on the** 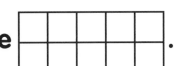 .
Subtract.

 5   9 – 2 = _____

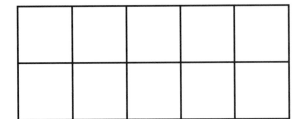

⭐ **6**   10 – 4 = _____

© 2020 Marshall Cavendish Education Pte Ltd

Count back to subtract.
Fill in each blank.

 7 How many frogs are left sitting?

6 − 2 = _____

There are _____ frogs left.

© 2020 Marshall Cavendish Education Pte Ltd

How many umbrellas are open?

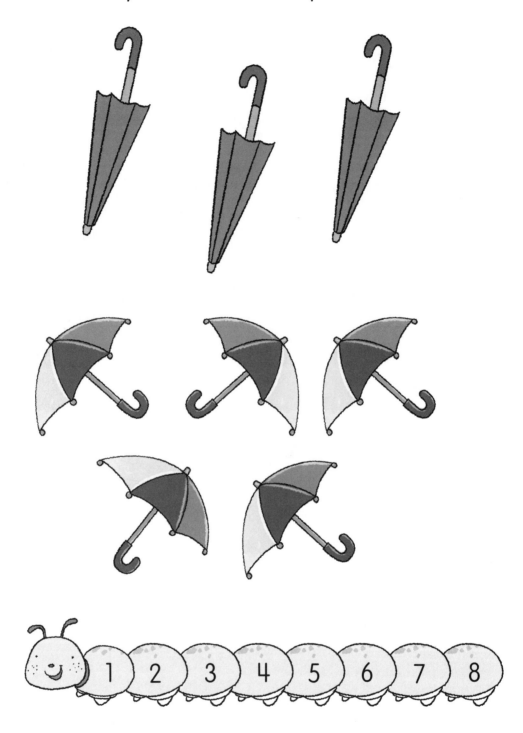

$8 - 3 =$ _____

_____ umbrellas are open.

© 2020 Marshall Cavendish Education Pte Ltd

9 How many chicks are **not** eating?

7 – _____ = _____

_____ chicks are **not** eating.

© 2020 Marshall Cavendish Education Pte Ltd

10 How many turtles are swimming?

9 – _____ = _____

_____ turtles are swimming.

© 2020 Marshall Cavendish Education Pte Ltd

How many rabbits hop away?

_____ – _____ = _____

_____ rabbits hop away.

Count back to subtract.
Fill in each blank.

12 7 – 3 = _____

© 2020 Marshall Cavendish Education Pte Ltd

13   9 – 4 = _____

---

 14   8 – 2 = _____

---

15   10 – 3 = _____

© 2020 Marshall Cavendish Education Pte Ltd

Chapter 8

Extra Practice and Homework
Subtraction

Activity 5   Subtraction Sentences

Solve.
Fill in each blank.

 There are 7 bees.

5 bees fly to collect honey.
How many bees are still in the tree?

7 – _____ = _____

_____ bees are still in the tree.

© 2020 Marshall Cavendish Education Pte Ltd

2 There are 7 crabs.
3 crabs are in the water.
How many crabs are **not** in the water?

7 – _____ = _____

_____ crabs are **not** in the water.

---

3 There are 8 children in the bus.
3 children are standing.
How many children are sitting?

8 – _____ = _____

_____ children are sitting.

© 2020 Marshall Cavendish Education Pte Ltd

4 There are 5 carrots in a basket.
Ms. Megan packs 3 carrots in a bag.
How many carrots are left in the basket?

_____ − 3 = _____

There are _____ carrots left in the basket.

---

5 Jose has 10 candles on his birthday cake.
He blows out 3 candles.
How many lighted candles are left on the cake?

10 − _____ = _____

There are _____ lighted candles left on the cake.

© 2020 Marshall Cavendish Education Pte Ltd

There are 9 monkeys.
1 monkey climbs down the tree.
How many monkey are still on the trees?

_____ – 1 = _____

_____ monkeys are still on the trees.

© 2020 Marshall Cavendish Education Pte Ltd

There are 8 butterflies.
2 butterflies fly away.
How many butterflies are left?

_____ – _____ = _____

There are _____ butterflies left.

© 2020 Marshall Cavendish Education Pte Ltd

There are 9 erasers in all.
5 erasers are circles.
How many erasers are **not** circles?

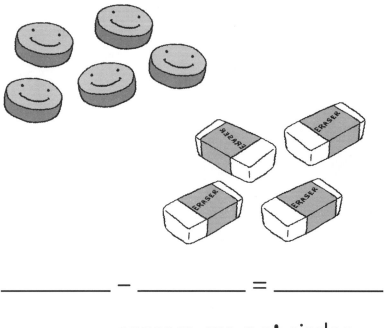

_____ – _____ = _____

_____ erasers are **not** circles.

© 2020 Marshall Cavendish Education Pte Ltd

Match the correct subtraction sentence.

   •   • $7 - 4 = 3$

   •   • $8 - 0 = 8$

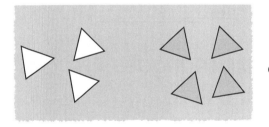   •   • $9 - 3 = 6$

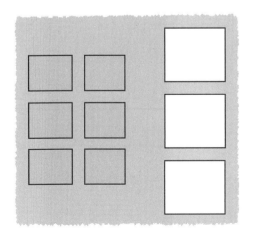   •   • $10 - 2 = 8$

© 2020 Marshall Cavendish Education Pte Ltd

9 Ms. Hall buys 7 mangoes.
4 mangoes are small.
How many big mangoes are there?

_____ – _____ = _____

There are _____ big mangoes.

© 2020 Marshall Cavendish Education Pte Ltd

Name: _____ Date: _____

Mathematical Habit 1 **Persevere in solving problems**

 1 Fill in each blank.

a Ms. White makes 10 glasses of juice.

She serves 8 glasses to her guests.
How many glasses of juice are left?

_____ – _____ = _____

There are _____ glasses of juice left.

b Draw the glasses of juice left.

┌─────────────────────────────────────┐
│   │
│   │
│   │
│   │
│   │
│   │
│   │
└─────────────────────────────────────┘

© 2020 Marshall Cavendish Education Pte Ltd

2 | **Mathematical Habit** **2** **Use mathematical reasoning**

Jacob bakes some .

He packs some for his friends.

Draw to show the story.

Jacob bakes _____ .

He packs _____ for his friends.

_____ − _____ = _____

There are _____ left with Jacob.

© 2020 Marshall Cavendish Education Pte Ltd

Mathematical Habit 6 Use precise mathematical language

1 Look at the picture.
Make three subtraction stories.

Write a subtraction sentence for each story.

_____ – _____ = _____

_____ – _____ = _____

_____ – _____ = _____

© 2020 Marshall Cavendish Education Pte Ltd

PUT ON YOUR THINKING CAP!

2 Look at the picture.

Make an ✗ on the subtraction sentence that does not belong.

10 − 7 = 3   5 − 1 = 4

8 − 5 = 3   7 − 5 = 2

© 2020 Marshall Cavendish Education Pte Ltd

SCHOOL-to-HOME
CONNECTIONS

Chapter 9

Numbers to 100

Dear Family,

In this chapter, your child will work with numbers to 100. Skills your child will practice include:

- counting to 100 by ones
- making 10s to count to 100
- finding the missing numbers in a number pattern

Math Activities

At the end of this chapter, you may want to carry out these activities with your child. These activities will help to support your child as he or she learns numbers to 100.

Activity 1

- Take a walk together to count 100 of something, such as 100 steps or 100 pebbles on a path. Or count 100 objects, such as 100 paper cups, 100 paper clips, or 100 pieces of macaroni.

Activity 2

- Visit a library and read books about 100, such as 100 *Snowmen* by Jen Arena, and *One Is a Snail, Ten Is a Crab: A Counting by Feet Book* by April Pulley Sayre and Jeff Sayre.

Math Talk

Make or go online to print a free hundreds chart as shown below. Gather several pennies or nickels, whichever coin covers the numbers in the chart completely, or use counters or checkers from game sets. Cover several squares on the chart. Ask your child to identify the numbers that are covered and count aloud. Play for a few rounds, covering different squares each time.

1	2	3	4	5	6	7	8	9	10
11	12	13	14	15	16	17	18	19	20
21	22	23	24	25	26	27	28	29	30
31	32	33	34	35	36	37	38	39	40
41	42	43	44	45	46	47	48	49	50
51	52	53	54	55	56	57	58	59	60
61	62	63	64	65	66	67	68	69	70
71	72	73	74	75	76	77	78	79	80
81	82	83	84	85	86	87	88	89	90
91	92	93	94	95	96	97	98	99	100

© 2020 Marshall Cavendish Education Pte Ltd

Activity 3

- Use sidewalk chalk to draw a hopscotch pattern on a flat surface. Write the numbers 10 to 100 in multiples of 10 inside the pattern as shown below. Toss a pebble, button, or some other objects and call out the numbers as you hop. Then, let your child play the next round.

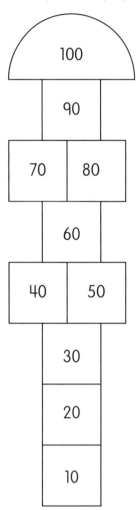

© 2020 Marshall Cavendish Education Pte Ltd

Chapter 9

Extra Practice and Homework
Numbers to 100

Activity 1   Numbers 21 to 50

Circle groups of 10.
Next, count on.
Then, color each correct number.

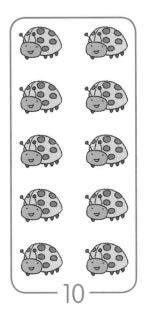  

| 25 | 27 | 28 |

© 2020 Marshall Cavendish Education Pte Ltd

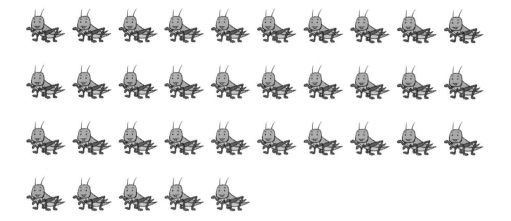

2

33	35	37

3

23	33	43

Extra Practice and Homework Grade KB

© 2020 Marshall Cavendish Education Pte Ltd

4

| 46 | 49 | 50 |

5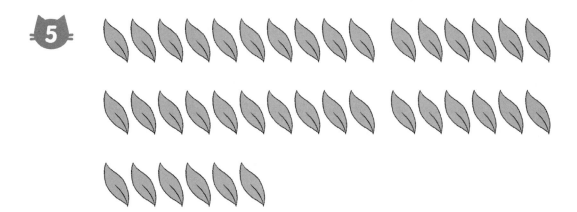

| 38 | 35 | 33 |

© 2020 Marshall Cavendish Education Pte Ltd

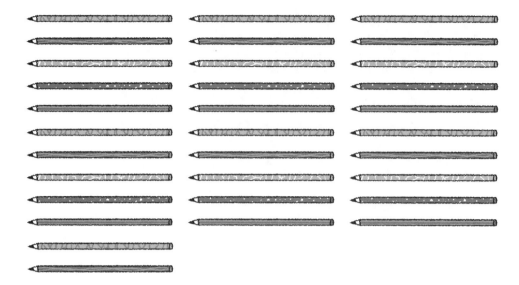

35   32   22

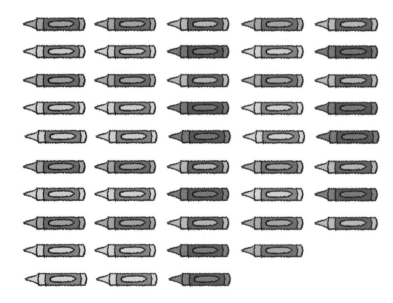

47   48   49

© 2020 Marshall Cavendish Education Pte Ltd

Color 26 .

© 2020 Marshall Cavendish Education Pte Ltd

Color 45 ♡.

© 2020 Marshall Cavendish Education Pte Ltd

Circle groups of 10.
Next, count on.
Then, match to the correct answer.

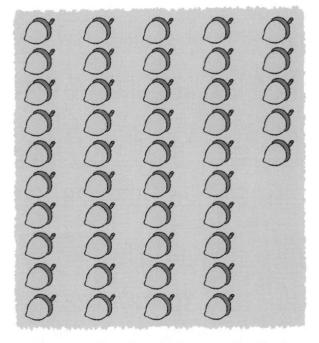

●   ● 23

●   ● 45

●   ● 31

© 2020 Marshall Cavendish Education Pte Ltd

Use the fifty chart to count.

1	2	3	4	5	6	7	8	9	10
11	12	13	14	15	16	17	18	19	20
21	22	23	24	25	26	27	28	29	30
31	32	33	34	35	36	37	38	39	40
41	42	43	44	45	46	47	48	49	50

a Count on from 11 to 28. Circle 28.

b Count on from 27 to 33. Color 33 red.

c Count back from 30 to 22. Make an ✗ on 22.

d Count back from 50 to 39. Color 39 blue.

© 2020 Marshall Cavendish Education Pte Ltd

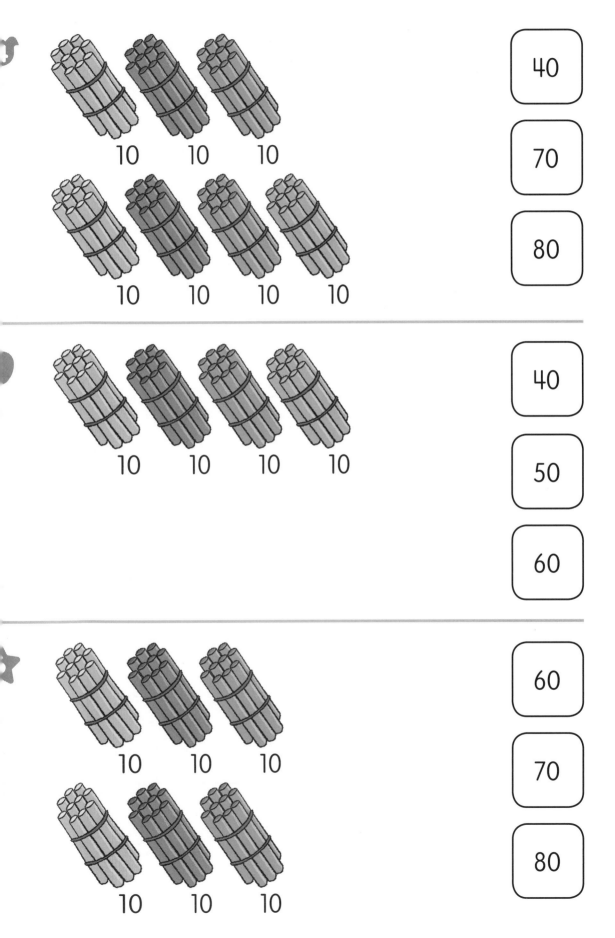

40

70

80

40

50

60

60

70

80

© 2020 Marshall Cavendish Education Pte Ltd

Chapter 9

Extra Practice and Hor
Numbers to 100

Activity 2 Count on by 10s to 100

Count on by 10s.
Color the box with the correct number.

 1

10

| 10 | 20 |

 2

10   10   10

| 30 | 40 |

 3

10   10

| 10 | 20 |

© 2020 Marshall Cavendish Education Pte Ltd

7

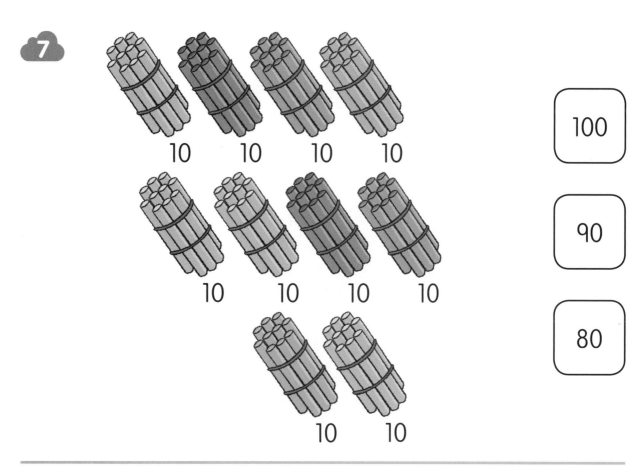

10 10 10 10

10 10 10 10

10 10

100

90

80

8

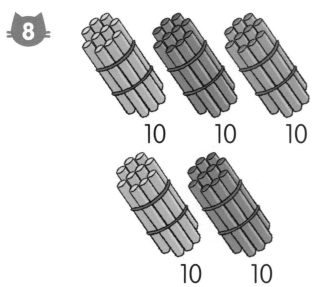

10 10 10

10 10

30

40

50

© 2020 Marshall Cavendish Education Pte Ltd

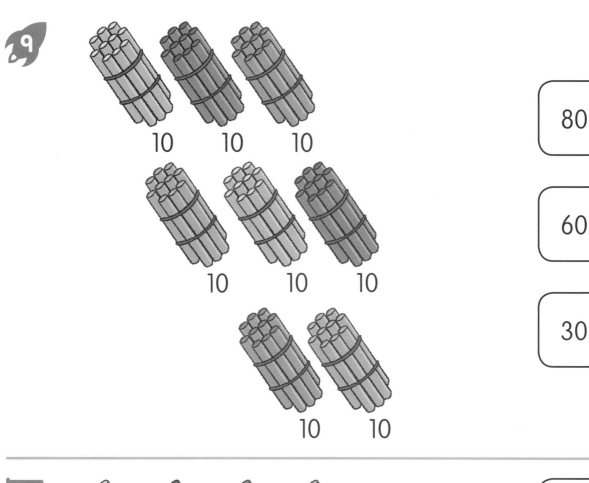

9

10   10   10

10   10   10

10   10

80

60

30

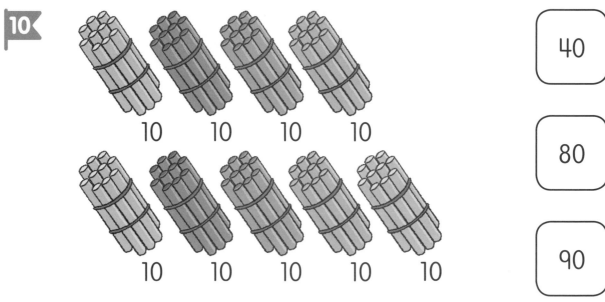

10

10   10   10   10

10   10   10   10   10

40

80

90

© 2020 Marshall Cavendish Education Pte Ltd

Count on by 10s.

Color the ⬡ with the correct number.

11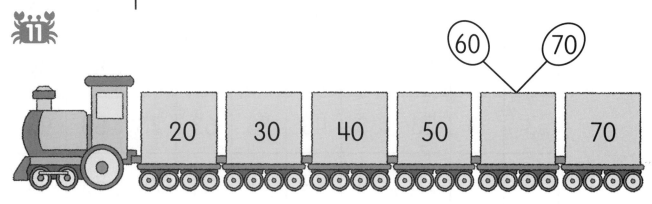

12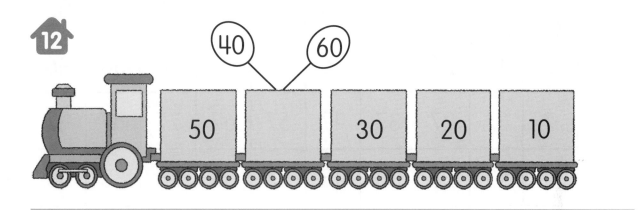

13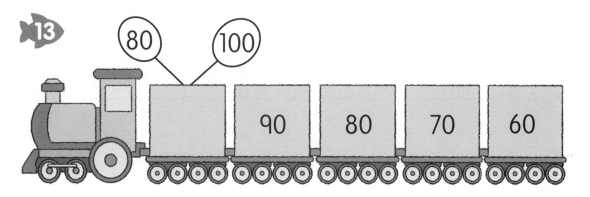

© 2020 Marshall Cavendish Education Pte Ltd

Count on by 10s.
Color the numbers you count green.

1	11	21	31	41	51	61	71	81	91
2	12	22	32	42	52	62	72	82	92
3	13	23	33	43	53	63	73	83	93
4	14	24	34	44	54	64	74	84	94
5	15	25	35	45	55	65	75	85	95
6	16	26	36	46	56	66	76	86	96
7	17	27	37	47	57	67	77	87	97
8	18	28	38	48	58	68	78	88	98
9	19	29	39	49	59	69	79	89	99
10	20	30	40	50	60	70	80	90	100

© 2020 Marshall Cavendish Education Pte Ltd

Chapter 9

Extra Practice and Homework
Numbers to 100

Activity 3   Numbers 51 to 100

Count on by groups of 10.
Next, count on.
Then, color the box with the correct number.

10

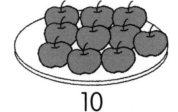

10

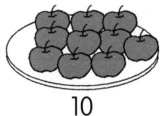

10

10

10

| 50 | 54 | 60 |

© 2020 Marshall Cavendish Education Pte Ltd

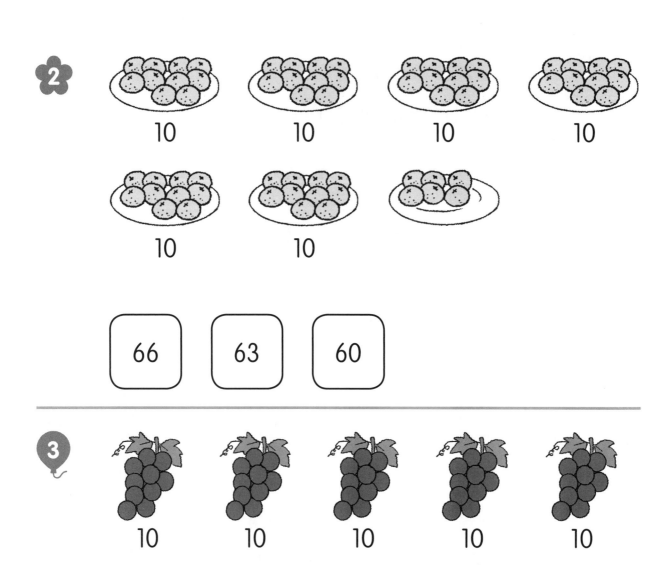

2

10　　10　　10　　10

10　　10

| 66 | 63 | 60 |

3

10　　10　　10　　10　　10

10　　10　　10　　10

| 100 | 98 | 97 |

© 2020 Marshall Cavendish Education Pte Ltd

4

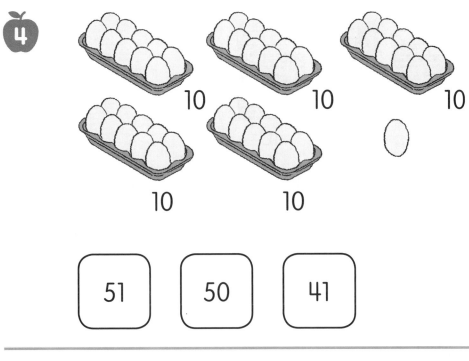

10   10   10

10   10

| 51 | 50 | 41 |

5

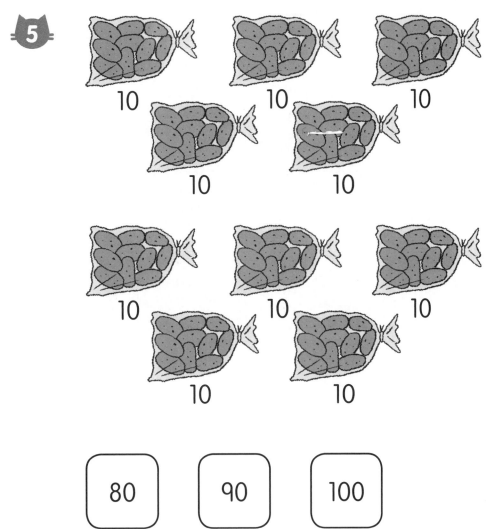

10   10   10

10   10

10   10   10

10   10

| 80 | 90 | 100 |

© 2020 Marshall Cavendish Education Pte Ltd

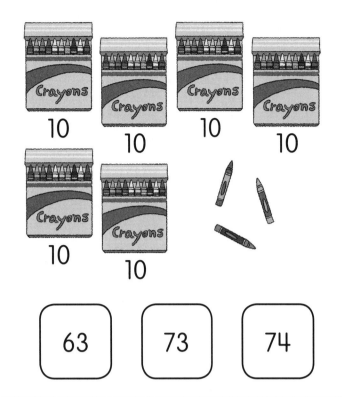

10 10 10 10
10 10

63   73   74

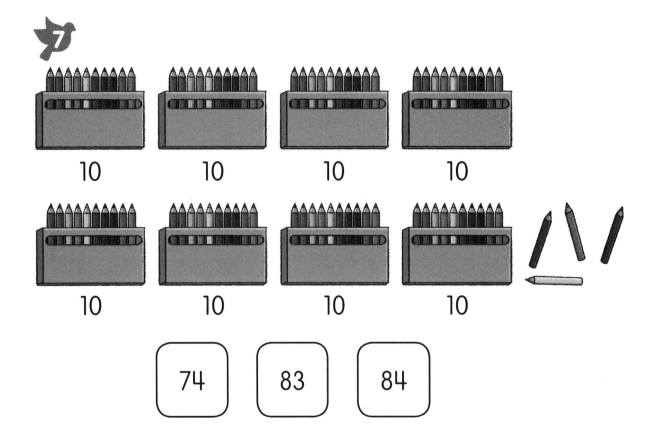

10 10 10 10
10 10 10 10

74   83   84

© 2020 Marshall Cavendish Education Pte Ltd

🚀 **8**

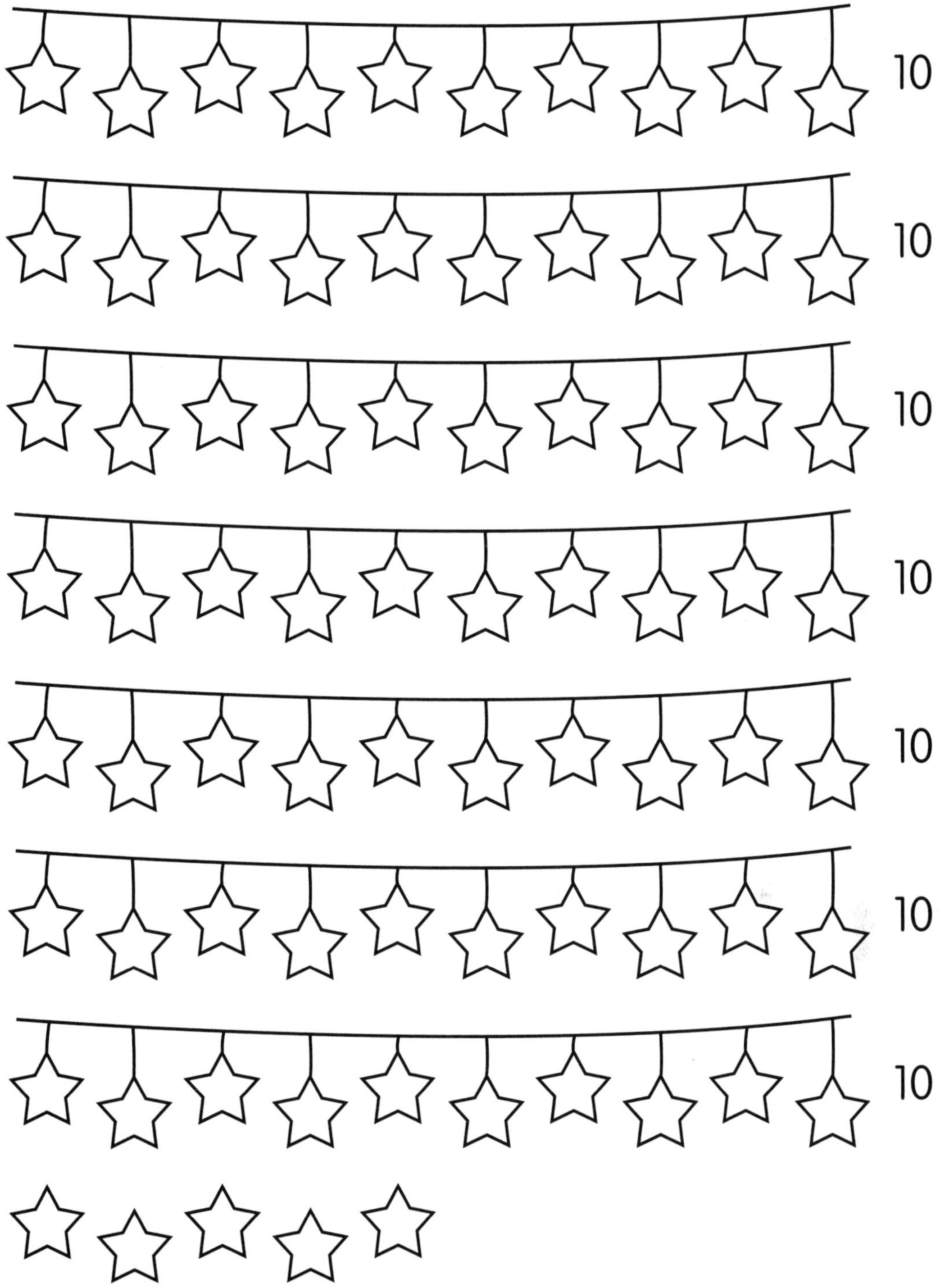

⭐⭐⭐⭐⭐⭐⭐⭐⭐⭐ 10

⭐⭐⭐⭐⭐⭐⭐⭐⭐⭐ 10

⭐⭐⭐⭐⭐⭐⭐⭐⭐⭐ 10

⭐⭐⭐⭐⭐⭐⭐⭐⭐⭐ 10

⭐⭐⭐⭐⭐⭐⭐⭐⭐⭐ 10

⭐⭐⭐⭐⭐⭐⭐⭐⭐⭐ 10

⭐⭐⭐⭐⭐⭐⭐⭐⭐⭐ 10

⭐⭐⭐⭐⭐

| 75 | 70 | 85 |

© 2020 Marshall Cavendish Education Pte Ltd

Use the hundred chart to count.

1	2	3	4	5	6	7	8	9	10
11	12	13	14	15	16	17	18	19	20
21	22	23	24	25	26	27	28	29	30
31	32	33	34	35	36	37	38	39	40
41	42	43	44	45	46	47	48	49	50
51	52	53	54	55	56	57	58	59	60
61	62	63	64	65	66	67	68	69	70
71	72	73	74	75	76	77	78	79	80
81	82	83	84	85	86	87	88	89	90
91	92	93	94	95	96	97	98	99	100

a Count on from 51 to 75. Color [75] blue.

b Count back from 100 to 83. Circle [83].

c Count on from 79 to 87. Make an **X** on [87].

© 2020 Marshall Cavendish Education Pte Ltd

Count on or count back.
Circle the correct number.

10   85, 86, 87, 88,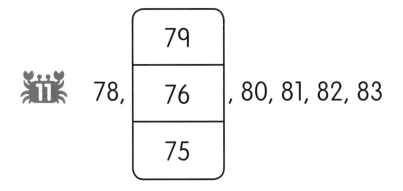

| 84 |
| 89 |
| 90 |

11   78, 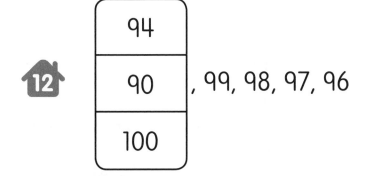 , 80, 81, 82, 83

| 79 |
| 76 |
| 75 |

12 | 94 |
| 90 | , 99, 98, 97, 96
| 100 |

© 2020 Marshall Cavendish Education Pte Ltd

Connect the dots.

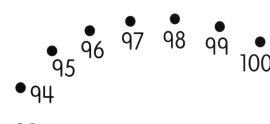

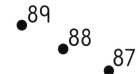

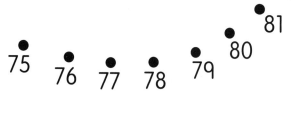

95 96 97 98 99 100

94

93

92

91

90

89

88

87

86

85

84

83

82

81

80

75 76 77 78 79

tar

© 2020 Marshall Cavendish Education Pte Ltd

Extra Practice and Homework Grade KB

Chapter 9

Extra Practice and Homework
Numbers to 100

Activity 4   Number Patterns

Count.
Complete each number pattern.

 1

 11   13 15 16

2

 20    17  16

3

13 14 16 17

4

 15 14   12

© 2020 Marshall Cavendish Education Pte Ltd

Look at each number pattern.
Color the box to complete each sentence.

12
14

comes right before 13.

17
19

comes right before 18.

17
19

comes right after 18.

© 2020 Marshall Cavendish Education Pte Ltd

each blank.

5	6		8		10

10			13	14	

17	16	15		13	

20	19			16	

© 2020 Marshall Cavendish Education Pte Ltd

1 less than 27 is

28
26

.

1 more than 27 is

28
26

.

22
24

is 1 less than 23.

22
24

is 1 more than 23.

© 2020 Marshall Cavendish Education Pte Ltd

Mathematical Habit 2 Use mathematical reasoning

Count the .

Circle to show how you count.

There are _____ .

© 2020 Marshall Cavendish Education Pte Ltd

Mathematical Habit 1 **Persevere in solving problems**

 Jack has five cards.
He wants to make a number pattern.

Three of his cards are 16 , 17 and 19 .

What are the other two cards?

His other two cards are [ ] and [ ].

© 2020 Marshall Cavendish Education Pte Ltd

Jack buys one more card for his pattern.
Which of these is the new card?
Make an ✗ on it.

Tell your partner why you say so.

© 2020 Marshall Cavendish Education Pte Ltd

BLANK

SCHOOL-to-HOME CONNECTIONS

Sorting

Dear Family,

In this chapter, your child will learn about sorting. Skills your child will practice include:
- identifying objects that are the same and objects that are different
- sorting objects into groups by color, count, shape, and size

Math Practice

At the end of this chapter, you may want to carry out these activities with your child. These activities will help to support your child as he or she learns about using attributes to classify and sort objects.

Activity 1
- Gather some colorful objects, such as buttons, beads, marbles, or building blocks.
- Ask your child to sort the objects by color.

Activity 2
- Gather some colorful pipe cleaners and cut them into different lengths.
- Ask your child to sort the pieces of pipe cleaners by color and then by length.

Activity 3
- Take a walk together and collect some natural objects, such as stones, leaves, and pine cones.
- Ask your child to sort the objects by color, shape, length, and weight.

Math Talk

Ask your child to gather a few toys. Look at the toys and talk about how they are the same and how they are different. For example, let's say you compare 2 trucks. Each truck has 4 wheels, which makes them the same. But one truck is red, and the other is blue, which makes them different. Think of other attributes, or characteristics, you can use to compare the toys, such as **colour**, **shape**, and **size** together with your child.

© 2020 Marshall Cavendish Education Pte Ltd

BLANK

Chapter 10
Extra Practice and Homework
Sorting

Activity 1 Same and Different

Which are the same?
Circle them.

© 2020 Marshall Cavendish Education Pte Ltd

4

5

6

© 2020 Marshall Cavendish Education Pte Ltd

Which is different?
Make an X on it.

 7

 8

© 2020 Marshall Cavendish Education Pte Ltd

9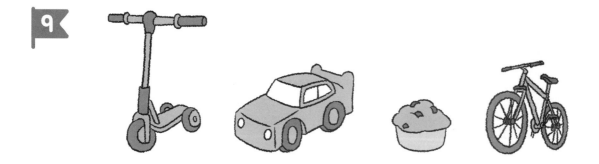

10

11

© 2020 Marshall Cavendish Education Pte Ltd

Chapter 10
Extra Practice and Homework
Sorting

Activity 2   Sort Objects by Attributes

Color and cut the fruits on page 181.
Sort by color and glue them below.
Count and write the number in each blank.

 1

_____	_____

© 2020 Marshall Cavendish Education Pte Ltd

Cut the pictures on page 181.
Sort by color and glue them below.
Count and write the number in each blank.

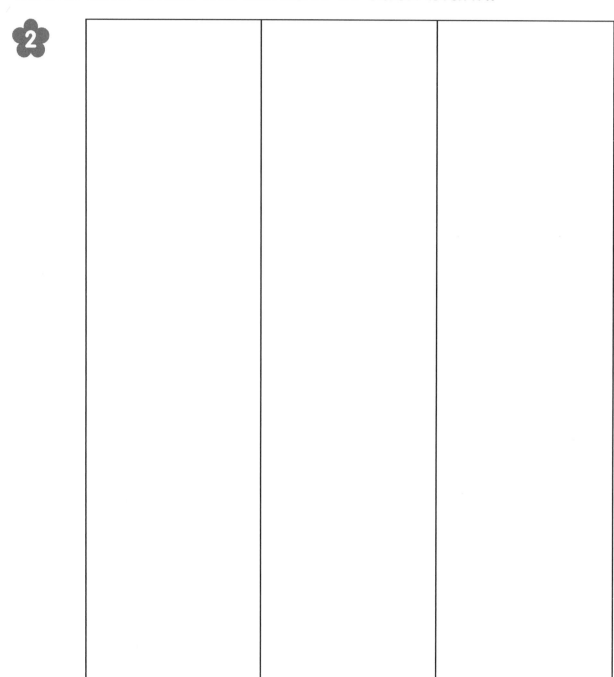

Color some balloons on page 183 green.
Color the rest yellow.
Sort by color and glue them below.

© 2020 Marshall Cavendish Education Pte Ltd

Sort by counting.
Make an X on the group of shapes that do not belong.

 4

 5

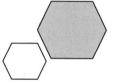 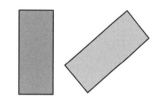

  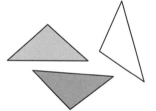

 6

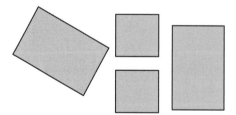 

Extra Practice and Homework Grade KB

© 2020 Marshall Cavendish Education Pte Ltd

Cut the pictures on page 185.
Sort by counting and glue them below.

Cut the pictures on page 183.
Sort by counting and glue them below.

7

© 2020 Marshall Cavendish Education Pte Ltd

Cut the pictures on page 185.
Sort by shape and glue them below.
Count and write the number in each blank.

_____	_____

© 2020 Marshall Cavendish Education Pte Ltd

Sort the shapes.
Color all ◯ red.

Color all △ blue.

Color all ☐ green.

Count.
Fill in each blank.

10

There are _____ ◯.

There are _____ △.

There are _____ ☐.

Cut the pictures on page 187.
Sort them by shape and glue them below.
Count and write the number in each blank.

© 2020 Marshall Cavendish Education Pte Ltd

Make an *X* on the shapes that do not belong.

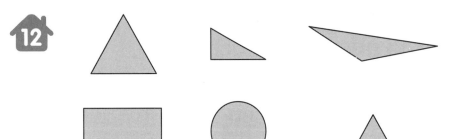

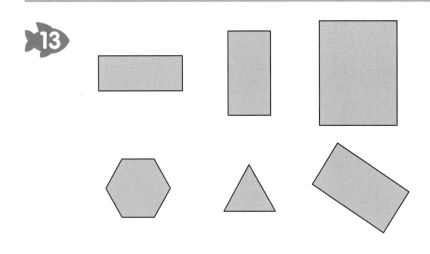

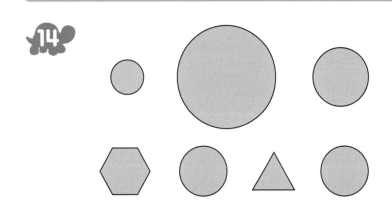

Cut the picture on page 187.
Sort them by size and glue them below.
Count and write each number in the blank.

© 2020 Marshall Cavendish Education Pte Ltd

Cut the pictures on page 189.
Sort them by size and glue them below.
Count and write each number in the blank.

16

_____	_____

Match.

 small

 big

square

circle

triangle

© 2020 Marshall Cavendish Education Pte Ltd

BLANK

MATH JOURNAL

Mathematical Habit 6 **Use precise mathematical language**

Look around your classroom.
How can you sort the objects?
You may use the words in the box.

table	book	sharpener
chair	pencil	globe
desk	crayon	balls
cupboard	ruler	paper
shelf	eraser	drawing
color	size	shape

Tell your partner about your groups.

© 2020 Marshall Cavendish Education Pte Ltd

Mathematical Habit 2 Use mathematical reasoning

 Cut the pictures on the next page.
Sort them and glue them below.
How did you sort them?
Tell your partner about it.

© 2020 Marshall Cavendish Education Pte Ltd

BLANK

Mathematical Habit 6 Use precise mathematical language

Luke is thinking of things of the same shape as the ball next to him.

Can you help Luke by pasting the photo of things of the same shape?

© 2020 Marshall Cavendish Education Pte Ltd

BLANK

For  on page 161.

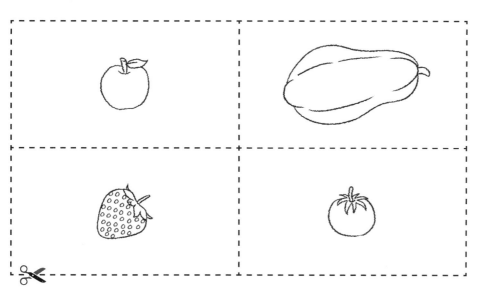

For 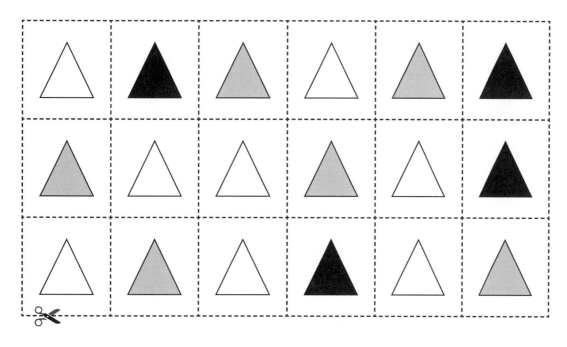 on page 162.

© 2020 Marshall Cavendish Education Pte Ltd

BLANK

For 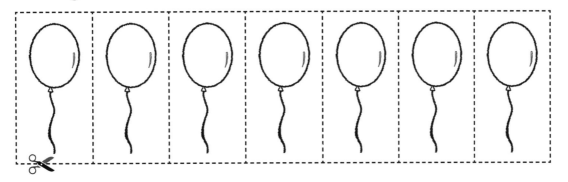 3 on page 163.

For 7 on page 165.

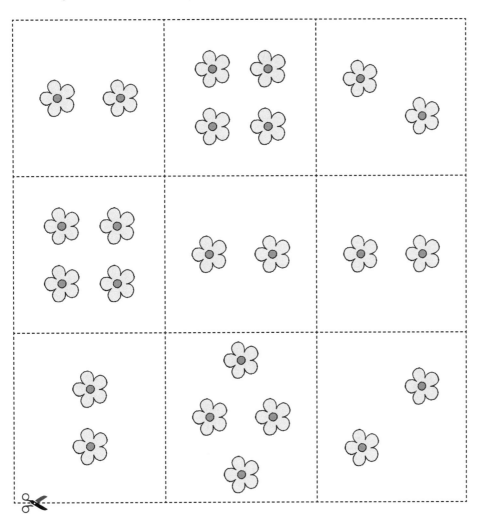

© 2020 Marshall Cavendish Education Pte Ltd

BLANK

For  on page 166.

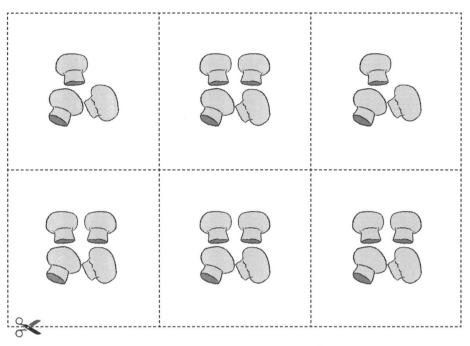

For 9 on page 167.

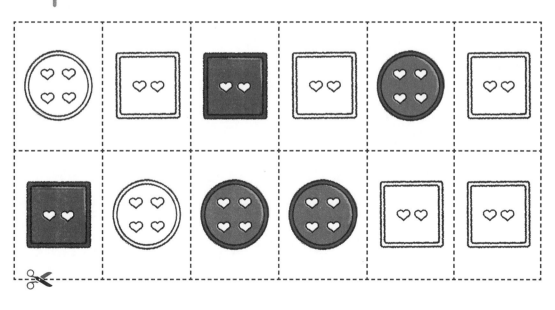

© 2020 Marshall Cavendish Education Pte Ltd

BLANK

BLANK

BLANK

M000026690

NSC
Bloodborne &
Airborne Pathogens

WORKBOOK

10M042319

Interior design, layout and composition and cover design: Bending Design Inc.

Photo Credits: Cover: © George Doyle/Stockbyte, © iStockphoto, © Photodisc/Thinkstock, © Siri Stafford Collection: Digital Vision, Page 14: © CDC/Dr. Thomas F. Sellers/Emory University. All other photographs © National Safety Council/Rick Brady, Photographer.

COPYRIGHT, WAIVER OF FIRST SALE DOCTRINE

National Safety Council materials are fully protected by the United States copyright laws and are solely for the noncommercial, internal use of the purchaser. Without the prior written consent of the National Safety Council, purchaser agrees that such materials shall not be rented, leased, loaned, sold, transferred, assigned, broadcast in any media form, publicly exhibited or used outside the organization of the purchaser or reproduced, stored in a retrieval system or transmitted in any form or by any means, electronic, mechanical, photocopying, recording or otherwise. Use of these materials for training for which compensation is received is prohibited, unless authorized by the National Safety Council in writing.

DISCLAIMER

Although the information and recommendations contained in this publication have been compiled from sources believed to be reliable, the National Safety Council makes no guarantee as to, and assumes no responsibility for, the correctness, sufficiency or completeness of such information or recommendations. Other or additional safety measures may be required under particular circumstances.

NATIONAL SAFETY COUNCIL MISSION STATEMENT

The National Safety Council saves lives by preventing injuries and deaths at work, in homes and communities, and on the roads, through leadership, research, education and advocacy.

nsc.org

© 2012 National Safety Council
       All Rights Reserved
       Printed in the U.S.A.

ISBN: 978-0-87912-315-4

About The National Safety Council

The National Safety Council is a nonprofit organization whose mission is to save lives by preventing injuries and deaths at work, in homes and communities and on the road through leadership, research, education and advocacy. NSC advances this mission by partnering with businesses, government agencies, elected officials and the public to make an impact where the most preventable injuries and deaths occur, in areas such as distracted driving, teen driving, workplace safety and beyond the workplace, particularly in and near our homes.

Founded in 1913 and chartered by Congress, the National Safety Council relies on research to determine optimal solutions to safety issues. Its educational efforts aim to change behaviors by building awareness, providing training and sharing best practices. The Council recognizes organizations that have focused on safety as a critical part of their operational excellence with the Robert W. Campbell Award®, safety's most prestigious honor. NSC Congress & Expo is the world's largest annual event dedicated to safety and *Safety+Health*® magazine is a leading source of occupational safety information. Offering a variety of learning options, NSC is a leader in First Aid and Workplace Safety training and created the defensive driving course concept where it remains the chief innovator. Each year the Green Cross for Safety® medal from NSC salutes a company with an outstanding safety record for its leadership in responsible citizenship and community service. The World Health Organization named NSC as the designated U.S. certification center for Safe Communities America®.

The National Safety Council is committed to helping its members and the public prevent unintentional injuries and deaths by providing knowledge and resources that enable them to reduce risks, engage employees, measure progress and continuously improve their safety management systems. With local Chapters and global networks, NSC is the leading advocate for safety and promotes June as National Safety Month.

Author Acknowledgments

Many National Safety Council staff and affiliates have contributed to the production of this book, and we would like to acknowledge the following people for their assistance:

Paul Satterlee, MD, for reviewing and providing oversight of content.

Donna M. Siegfried, Senior Director, First Aid Programs, for providing vision and support.

Barbara Caracci, Director, Program Development and Training, First Aid Programs, for providing technical writing services and oversight of development processes and production.

Donna Fredenhagen, Product Manager, First Aid Programs, for providing marketing support.

Kathy Safranek, Project Administrator, for providing day-to-day assistance.

Roseann Solak, Manager, Product Development, for oversight management of development processes and design teams.

Pauline DePinto, Project Manager, for coordinating development and production.

The Council also recognizes with appreciation the many other NSC employees who devoted time to this project.

Reviewer Acknowledgments

Lorri Greenlee, RN, BSN, MHCL
Coordinator of Health Services
USD 465, Winfield Public Schools
Winfield, KS

Deb Kaye, BS, NREMT
Director/Instructor EMS
Dakota County Technical College
Rosemount, MN

Paul Reynolds, EMT
Battalion Chief
Gila River EMS
Sacaton, AZ

Cindy Tait, RN, EMT-P, CEN, PHN, MPH
President
Center for Healthcare Education, Inc.
Riverside, CA

Table of Contents

Lesson 1 • Introduction to the Bloodborne Pathogens Standard

Lesson Preview

- Overview
- Employees Protected
- Other Requirements

- Other Regulations
- Required Training

The United States Occupational Safety and Health Administration (OSHA) creates and enforces safety standards for workplaces. **The Occupational Exposure to Bloodborne Pathogens Standard (the Standard)** was designed to eliminate or minimize employees' exposure to human blood and **other potentially infectious materials (OPIM)** in the workplace. The Standard went into effect in 1992 and applies to all employees who, as part of their job, may reasonably expect to be exposed to blood and OPIM that may contain pathogens.

Overview

Pathogens are germs that cause disease. **Bloodborne pathogens** are germs transmitted from one person to another through contact with blood or OPIM. OPIM include human body fluids and anything contaminated by them. **Lesson 2** contains a listing of body fluids that are potentially infectious. The Standard applies to employees who may be at risk even if their jobs for the most part do not involve giving first aid or working near or with bloodborne pathogens **(Figure 1-1)**.

The United States Centers for Disease Control and Prevention (CDC) also provides guidelines for preventing exposure to bloodborne

Figure 1-1 *The OSHA Bloodborne Standard protects employees in many different occupations.*

pathogens. Practices and procedures from both organizations are included in this workbook.

Practices described in this workbook also meet the required education and training standards of the National Fire Protection Association (NFPA) for infection control. Additional recommendations for infection control programs for fire departments can be found in NFPA 1581(http://www.nfpa.org).

Who Does the Standard Protect?

The Standard protects full-time, part-time and temporary employees whose job involves handling or possibly being exposed to blood or blood products, blood components or OPIM. This includes but is not limited to:

- Airline mechanics
- Animal handlers
- Athletic trainers
- Clinical technicians
- Correctional officers
- Custodians
- Dentists and other dental workers
- EMS providers **(Figure 1-2)**

- Engineering staff
- Firefighters
- Health care workers
- Housekeeping personnel
- Hospice employees
- Law enforcement personnel
- Lifeguards
- Massage therapists
- Modification practitioners (tattoo and body piercing artists)
- Morticians
- Physical therapists
- Research technicians
- Veterinarians
- Waste collectors

OSHA estimates that millions of workers in health care and related occupations are at risk for occupational exposure to bloodborne pathogens. The CDC estimates that 3.5-5.3 million people, 1-2% of the United States population, are living with chronic hepatitis B virus (HBV) or hepatitis C virus (HCV) infections. Of those, 800,000 to 1.4 million have chronic HBV infections and 2.7-3.9 million have chronic HCV infections.[1]

You do not need to directly contact someone carrying a bloodborne pathogen to be at risk for exposure. Employees who perform job tasks such as handling clinical specimens, biohazardous trash, blood or body-fluid-soaked laundry or needles or other sharps should also have bloodborne pathogens training. It is the

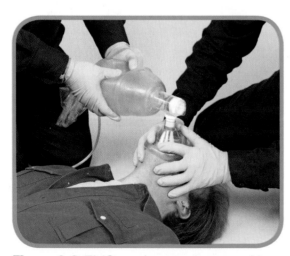

Figure 1-2 *EMS workers are covered by the Standard.*

[1]*(http://www.cdc.gov/hepatitis/PDFs/IOM-Hepatitis AndLiverCancerReport.pdf Accessed 09/16/11)*

employer's responsibility to determine which job classifications or specific tasks and procedures involve occupational exposure.

Who Is Excluded from the Standard?

The construction industry is not covered by the Standard. However, OSHA's General Duty Clause (Section 5(a) (1)) is used to protect employees from bloodborne pathogens in construction.

The Standard does not cover people who give first aid as **Good Samaritans.** This is first aid a person voluntarily gives to another person, such as performing CPR or helping someone with a cut, nose bleed or other injury off the job. The Standard focuses on **occupational exposure,** which is specifically defined by OSHA as "a reasonably anticipated skin, eye, mucous membrane or parenteral contact with blood or OPIM that may result from the performance of employees' duties."

What Training Is Required?

The Standard requires that all employees who perform tasks involving potential occupational exposure to bloodborne pathogens receive initial and annual training. Initial training must be conducted prior to being placed in positions where occupational exposure may occur. Employees must be retrained at least once every 12 months (within a time period not to exceed 365 days), regardless of the employee's other training or education. Circumstances that warrant more frequent training may occur (e.g., when there are changes in workplace practices, procedures or tasks or when employee performance suggests the prior training was incomplete or not fully understood).

The training should cover the hazards employees face (how bloodborne diseases are transmitted and their symptoms), the protective measures they can take to prevent exposure and procedures to follow if they are exposed. Industry-specific and site-specific information must be included. Employers should tailor the training to the employee's background and responsibilities.

What Else Is Required by the Standard?

The Standard requires that, where appropriate, employers have a written Exposure Control Plan that clearly outlines how employees are to prevent exposures through engineering controls, work practice controls, universal precautions and personal protective equipment. The Plan must be accessible to employees as well as to OSHA and NIOSH representatives. These topics are covered in detail later in this workbook.

The Standard also requires recordkeeping. Recordkeeping for exposure incidents must comply with OSHA 29 CFR Part 1904 ("Recording and Reporting Occupational Injuries and Illnesses") or applicable State plan provisions, using OSHA Form 300 **(Figure 1-3)** and either OSHA Form 301 or the incident reporting form used by the organization. Records must be kept in accordance with the Health Insurance Portability and Accountability Act (HIPAA) and must be maintained for a minimum of 5 years. Copies of these forms can be obtained on OSHA's website at www.osha.gov.

Training records must be kept for 3 years from the date of training and should include the dates of the training sessions, the contents or a summary of the training, the names and qualifications of the people conducting the training and the names and job titles of all who attended the training session. A sample bloodborne pathogens training log is on page 58.

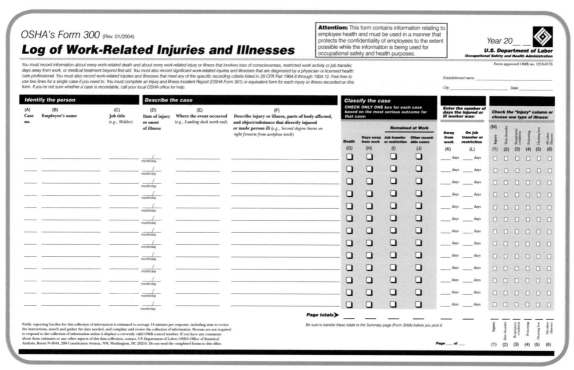

Figure 1-3 *Record exposure incidents on OSHA Form 300.*

Other Regulations

The Needlestick Safety and Prevention Act, which became effective in April 2001, requires employers to identify, evaluate and implement safer medical devices. The Act provides expanded protection for employees, including maintaining a sharps injury log that serves as a tool for identifying high-risk areas and evaluating devices. Employers are required to review the log both periodically and as part of the annual review and update of the Exposure Control Plan. Employers also are required to annually document their consideration and implementation of appropriate commercially available and effective safer medical devices and to involve non-management workers in evaluating and choosing them **(Figure 1-4).** Employers are given flexibility to solicit employee input in a manner appropriate to the circumstances of the workplace.

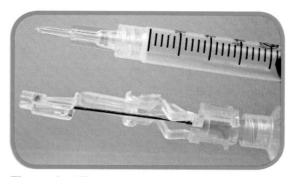

Figure 1-4 *To reduce the risk of accidental needlesticks from conventional syringes with needles, many employers are now using needleless devices and self-sheathing needles.*

Learning Checkpoint 1

1. True or False: The OSHA Bloodborne Pathogens Standard covers all employees who, in the course of their daily work, may reasonably expect to be exposed to blood or OPIM that may contain bloodborne pathogens.

2. True or False: Only health care workers are covered under the Bloodborne Pathogens Standard.

3. A Good Samaritan is –

   a. always covered by the Bloodborne Pathogens Standard.

   b. not covered by the Bloodborne Pathogens Standard.

   c. covered only when helping a coworker.

   d. covered only when on company property.

4. True or False: OSHA mandates that employees who may be exposed to bloodborne pathogens receive training every 5 years.

Lesson 2 • Bloodborne Pathogens

Lesson Preview

- Disease Transmission
- Bloodborne Pathogens
- Other Potentially Infectious Materials
- Hepatitis B
- Hepatitis C
- HIV

An occupational exposure to infected blood or OPIM can occur in many occupations. An occupational exposure puts you at risk for infection from disease-causing microorganisms and could result in hepatitis B, hepatitis C or HIV.

How Are Infectious Diseases Transmitted?

Preventing transmission of infectious disease is based on understanding how disease is transmitted **(Figure 2-1)**. This process involves 4 stages

1. ***The process begins with an infected individual.***

2. ***The infectious pathogen (disease-causing bacteria, virus, fungus or parasite) leaves the infected person's body.*** For example:

   - The person may bleed from a cut, and in that person's blood is the pathogen.

   - The person may sneeze or cough out little droplets carrying the pathogen.

3. ***The infectious pathogen reaches another person and enters his or her body.*** This can happen in a number of ways:

   - The person may come into contact with the infected person's blood, body fluid or

other infectious material in a way such that the pathogen enters his or her body through mucous membranes or non-intact skin **(bloodborne transmission).**

- The person may inhale the pathogen in tiny droplets in the air **(airborne transmission).**

- The person may be bitten by an insect, such as a tick or mosquito, carrying the pathogen **(vector transmission).**

Transmission of a pathogen from one person to another is said to occur through direct or in direct contact:

- **Direct contact** occurs with contact with an infected person or fluids or substances from that person.

- **Indirect contact** occurs with contact with contaminated objects, droplets in the air or vectors such as insects.

4. ***The second person develops the infection.*** Just having the pathogen enter the body

Figure 2-1 *Different modes of disease transmission.*

does not automatically mean a person will become ill. He or she may have been vaccinated against the disease, which helps protect the body by developing antibodies to kill or limit the pathogen's ability to cause the disease. A person's natural immune system may be able to kill some pathogens and thereby prevent illness. Or a person may become infected. The process then starts all over again.

What Are Bloodborne Pathogens?

Bloodborne pathogens are microorganisms that are present in human blood and can cause disease in humans. Common serious bloodborne pathogens that may be encountered in the workplace include, but are not limited to:

- Hepatitis B virus (HBV)
- Hepatitis C virus (HCV)
- Human immunodeficiency virus (HIV), which can lead to acquired immunodeficiency syndrome (AIDS)

Other diseases that may result from bloodborne pathogens are described at the end of this lesson.

Although the OSHA Occupational Exposure to Bloodborne Pathogens Standard (the Standard) covers all bloodborne pathogens, this workbook describes only HBV, HCV and HIV because these are the most common and serious pathogens you will likely come in contact with at work in the United States. Measures you take to prevent these infections will also help prevent diseases caused by other bloodborne pathogens.

What Other Substances Are Potentially Infectious?

Both blood and **other potentially infectious materials (OPIM)** may contain bloodborne pathogens. According to the Standard, OPIM may include these human body fluids and anything contaminated with them:

- Saliva containing blood (as in dental procedures)
- Semen
- Vaginal secretions
- Breast milk
- Amniotic fluid (the fluid in the uterus around the fetus)
- Cerebrospinal fluid (the fluid that surrounds the spinal cord and brain)
- Synovial fluid (the fluid in joints)
- Pleural fluid (the fluid between the linings of the lungs)
- Peritoneal fluid (the fluid contained in the abdomen)
- Pericardial fluid (the fluid surrounding heart)
- Any body fluid visibly contaminated with blood (such as vomit or urine)

OPIM may also include the following **(Figure 2-2):**

- Blood, organs or other tissue from experimental animals infected with HBV or HIV
- Tissue samples or organ cultures or cell cultures containing HIV
- Non-intact skin (acne, burns, rashes, etc.) or organs from a human
- HBV-containing cultures or other solutions

Do Exposures Always Cause Infection?

Exposures do not always cause infection. The risk of infection following an exposure to blood or another body fluid depends on many factors, including:

- Whether pathogens are present in the source blood or body fluid
- The number of pathogens present
- The type of injury or exposure – how the infectious material gets into your body
- Your current health and immunization status

This means even if the source person's blood or OPIM contain pathogens, you are not necessarily infected. To be safe, however, always assume an exposure is potentially infectious and follow all recommended measures to prevent exposures from occurring.

☣ ALERT!
UNKNOWN BODY FLUID

You must also take precautions in situations when it is not possible to identify a body fluid. Any unknown fluid suspected to be a body fluid should be handled according to OSHA standards.

Figure 2-2 *Potentially infectious materials include tissues and some lab animals.*

Learning Checkpoint 1

1. True or False: There are only 3 bloodborne pathogens: HBV, HCV and HIV.

2. True or False: Bloodborne pathogens are present in all human blood and will cause disease in people who have weak immune systems.

3. OPIM include: (Check all that apply.)

   _____ a. Saliva in dental procedures

   _____ b. Semen

   _____ c. Vaginal secretions

   _____ d. Bloody vomit

4. What other substances can contain bloodborne pathogens? (Check all that apply.)

   _____ a. HBV-containing cultures or other solutions

   _____ b. Breast milk

   _____ c. Tissue or organ cultures or cell cultures containing HIV

   _____ d. Animal blood

   _____ e. Vomit containing blood

Hepatitis

Hepatitis means inflammation of the liver and also refers to a group of viral infections that affect the liver. The most common types are hepatitis A, hepatitis B and hepatitis C.

Viral hepatitis is the leading cause of liver cancer and the most common reason for liver transplantation. An estimated 4.4 million Americans are living with chronic hepatitis; most do not know they are infected. About 80,000 new infections occur every year.[1]

Hepatitis B

Hepatitis B, also called serum hepatitis, is caused by the **hepatitis B virus (HBV)** HBV is transmitted by blood and OPIM. Although HBV has been found in all body secretions and excretions, blood and semen are the most infectious. HBV infections are a major cause of liver damage, cirrhosis and liver cancer. Because of routine hepatitis B vaccinations, the number of new infections per year has declined significantly, particularly in children and adolescents. However, the Centers for Disease Control and Prevention (CDC) reports that in the United States HBV still infects about 43,000 people yearly, and there are about 1.2 million chronic carriers in the population. It is estimated that 3,000 people die of liver problems associated with HBV infection every year.[2]

The time from exposure to developing HBV averages 120 days, with a range of 45-160 days. Infection by HBV can cause either

[1] *(http://www.cdc.gov/hepatitis/index.htm Accessed 09/15/11)*

[2] *(http://www.cdc.gov/hepatitis/Resources/Professionals /PDFs/ABCTable.pdf Accessed 09/15/11)*

acute hepatitis or a chronic (long-term) HBV infection, depending on how the body responds to the virus. In most cases the body produces an antibody that helps destroy liver cells that contain the virus, which eliminates the virus from the body. The person then has lifelong immunity to the hepatitis B virus. About 95% of adults who are infected develop antibodies and recover within 6 months of being infected. Once they recover, they are not infectious to others.

Those who do develop chronic HBV infections, however, do not develop the antibody and can carry the virus and be infectious to others for decades. A person who still has the virus 6 months after infection is considered chronically infected. Chronic infection can lead to severe liver damage and death.

How Is HBV Spread?

HBV is spread in the following ways:

- By injection (such as needlesticks or puncture wounds)
- Through mucous membranes (blood contamination through the eye or mouth) and non-intact skin (for example, abrasions or lacerations)
- Through sexual activity
- From infected mother to newborn at birth

The most likely mode of transmission of HBV is direct contact with infectious blood through a needlestick or injury by another sharp instrument. Health care workers face these risks in the work environment **(Figure 2-3).** With current blood testing, the blood supply today is generally safe, although a theoretical risk of infection remains with blood transfusions.

Exposure to HBV on contaminated environmental surfaces is another common mode of transmission. At room temperature the virus may survive for at least 1 week in dried body fluids on surfaces such as tables and faucets **(Figure 2-4).** HBV is easily transmitted because it can live longer than other pathogens outside the body and because very little blood is needed to cause infection. HBV can be spread by sharing such personal items as a razor, toothbrush or drug paraphernalia like needles and syringes.

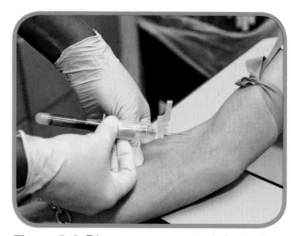

Figure 2-3 *Direct exposure to infected blood is the greatest risk for bloodborne disease.*

Figure 2-4 *HBV can live for many days on contaminated surfaces.*

HBV is not transmitted in food or water, in fecal matter, through the air or through casual contact with an infected person **(Figure 2-5).** Casual contact includes activities such as the following:

- Sharing a meal, utensils or a drinking glass
- Kissing, hugging or touching
- Being around someone who sneezes or coughs
- Sharing a phone or bathroom

Symptoms of HBV

About 30% of HBV-infected people have no symptoms. When symptoms do occur, they usually appear gradually and are often flu-like. These symptoms may include the following:

- Loss of appetite
- Nausea, vomiting
- Fatigue
- Muscle or joint aches
- Mild fever
- Stomach pain
- Occasionally jaundice (yellow tint to whites of eyes or skin)

ALERT!
HEPATITIS B VACCINATION

In the typical vaccination schedule, the second dose is generally given 1 month after the first, and the third dose 6 months after the first.

This schedule may vary depending on specific circumstances, but in all cases it is important to stay on the schedule as stated by the health care provider giving the vaccine.

How Do I Know If I Have HBV?

Because the symptoms vary so much, the only way to know for sure if you have HBV is to have your blood tested for hepatitis B. The blood test may not, however, indicate the presence of the virus shortly after infection.

Hepatitis B Vaccine

The hepatitis B vaccine is the best protection against HBV. In general, the CDC recommends the hepatitis B vaccination for all infants, older children and adolescents who were not vaccinated previously and for adults at risk for HBV infection. The vaccine is prepared from yeast cultures, not from human blood or plasma, and therefore there is no risk of contamination with other bloodborne pathogens or of developing hepatitis from the vaccine. Three doses of the vaccine are given by injection on 3 different dates. (In some situations more than 3 doses may be needed.) The most common adverse reaction to vaccination is soreness at the injection site.

The use of the hepatitis B vaccine along with environmental, engineering and work practice controls can prevent most workplace and occupational infections of HBV.

Figure 2-5 *Casual contact does not transmit HBV.*

In addition to employees at risk, the CDC also recommends that certain groups of people should get the hepatitis B vaccine including those who:

- Have unprotected sex with a partner who has HBV or who have sex with more than one partner.

- Have anal sex.

- Use intravenous (IV) recreational drugs.

- Are hemophiliacs.

- Frequently travel to or live in countries where HBV is common.

- Live with someone with chronic HBV.

The vaccine prevents hepatitis B in about 95% of people who get all 3 shots. After receiving all 3 shots, you can be tested to make certain you are protected. This is important if you have a compromised immune system or your job frequently exposes you to human blood.

The Standard requires employers to offer the hepatitis B vaccine to employees at risk for exposure at no cost, at a convenient time and place and during their normal work hours. If travel away from the work site is required, the employer is responsible for the travel cost.

As an employee, you have the right to refuse the vaccine. Common reasons for refusing the vaccine are:

(continues on page 13)

Learning Checkpoint 2

1. True or False: More than one blood test may be necessary in some cases to determine if a person has HBV.

2. True or False: An employer is required to provide the hepatitis B vaccine at no cost to employees at risk.

3. HBV may enter the body through – (Check all that apply.)

   _____ a. skin abrasions.

   _____ b. open cuts.

   _____ c. mucous membranes in the nose or mouth.

   _____ d. mucous membrances in the eyes.

4. Which of the following are the most likely body fluids to cause HBV infection? (Check all that apply.)

   _____ a. Semen

   _____ b. Vaginal secretions

   _____ c. Blood

   _____ d. Sweat

5. True or False: After about 2 years, a person who carries HBV is no longer infectious to others.

(continued from page 12)

- Documentation exists that you have previously received the hepatitis B series.

- Antibody testing shows you are immune.

- You are allergic to any component of the vaccine.

- Medical evaluation shows the vaccination is not adviseable.

If you choose not to be immunized, you will be asked to sign a declination form. You also have the right to change your mind at a later date and receive the vaccination. A sample declination form is on page 48.

Employers are required to:

- Offer training and the hepatitis B vaccine before employees start a work assignment.

- Explain to employees that vaccination is voluntary.

- Make certain employees receive proper medical treatment following any exposure incident, regardless of their vaccination history, and are offered the vaccination if they have not received it earlier.

Prevention of HBV Infection

The hepatitis B vaccine is the best way to prevent becoming infected with hepatitis B. If you choose not to be vaccinated, however, you can prevent infection by protecting yourself from exposure to blood and OPIM. These include the same protections you should take to avoid all bloodborne pathogens:

- Using barriers to prevent contact with any blood and OPIM

- Handling sharps with extreme care

- Avoiding recreational IV drugs

- Protected sexual contact

- Avoiding the sharing of contaminated needles, syringes or other injection drug equipment

- Avoiding tattooing and body piercing if the tools are not sterile

- Not sharing any personal care items that may be contaminated with blood

The next lesson discusses these guidelines in more detail.

Hepatitis C

Hepatitis C is a liver disease caused by the **hepatitis C virus (HCV).** This virus lives in the blood of people with the disease and is spread via the blood. The time from exposure to developing HCV averages 45 days with a range of 14-180 days. The CDC reports an estimated 3.2 million people in the United States have chronic HCV infection and about 17,000 new infections occur each year. HCV does not always cause serious health problems. Many people who carry HCV have some liver damage but do not feel sick from it. In others, cirrhosis of the liver may develop, resulting in eventual liver failure. The CDC estimates 12,000 people in the United States die from HCV-related illness per year.[3]

How Is HCV Spread?

In the general population, HCV spreads most often through sharing of contaminated needles, syringes or other injection drug equipment. HCV infection may also result from unclean tattoo or body piercing tools, improper disposal of body piercing tools or from sharing toothbrushes, razors or any other item contaminated with blood. HCV can also be transmitted from a pregnant woman to the fetus and, more rarely, through sexual contact.

[3](http://www.cdc.gov/hepatitis/Resources/Professionals/ PDFs/ABCTable.pdf Accessed 09/16/11)

For those employed in health care facilities, the primary risk of HCV transmission is by direct contact with infectious blood through an accidental needlestick or injury with other sharps.

Symptoms of HCV

Most people with hepatitis C do not have symptoms. However, some people may feel one or more of the following symptoms:

- Fatigue
- Loss of appetite
- Nausea
- Anxiety
- Weight loss
- Alcohol intolerance
- Abdominal pain
- Loss of concentration
- Jaundice **(Figure 2-6)**

How Do I Know If I Have HCV?

Several different blood tests can be done to determine if you have HCV. A false positive test (a test result appears positive when the person is not infected) can occur with HCV tests, however. Therefore, anyone who tests positive should have a follow-up test. False negative test results may also occur with HCV. These usually occur with testing done shortly after infection when antibodies have not yet developed and therefore cannot be accurately measured. A different type of blood test may then be recommended.

The CDC recommends HCV testing for the following groups of people:

- Health care workers who have been exposed to HCV-positive blood

- Anyone who has used recreational IV drugs
- Anyone who received a blood transfusion or organ transplant or was on kidney dialysis prior to 1992
- Anyone treated with a blood product prior to 1987
- Anyone with signs of liver disease

Testing is important for these people because, if necessary, treatment can be given to protect the liver from additional damage, and people who know they are HCV carriers can take preventive measures to avoid spreading HCV to others.

Prevention of HCV Infection

There currently is no vaccine available for HCV and no cure. Therefore, preventive measures are very important. The following are recommended preventive practices:

- Handle needles and other sharps with caution, and follow barrier practices to prevent contact with blood and OPIM **(Lesson 3).**

- Avoid recreational IV drug use, and never reuse or share syringes or drug paraphernalia.

(continues on page 15)

Figure 2-6 *Yellowish color of the whites of eyes may be a sign of jaundice.*

Learning Checkpoint 3

1. True or False: HCV can be spread through any exposure to saliva, sweat or semen.

2. True or False: The vaccine that prevents HBV is also effective for HCV.

3. Check off which symptoms may be present with HCV:

   _____a. Nausea   _____d. Loss of appetite

   _____b. Hair loss   _____e. Sores that do not heal

   _____c. Abdominal pain   _____f. Fatigue

4. True or False: HCV can cause eventual liver failure.

(continued from page 14)

- Do not share toothbrushes, razors or other personal care items that may be contaminated with blood **(Figure 2-7).**

- Remember the health risks associated with tattoos and body piercing if tools are not sterile or sanitary practices are not followed.

Human Immunodeficiency Virus and Acquired Immunodeficiency Syndrome

Human immunodeficiency virus (HIV) is the virus that can lead to **acquired immunodeficiency syndrome (AIDS).** There are 2 types of HIV: HIV-1 and HIV-2. In the United States, the term HIV primarily refers to HIV-1 because HIV-2 is largely confined to western Africa. Both types of HIV destroy specific blood cells, called CD4+T cells, which are crucial to helping the body fight diseases. AIDS is the late stage of HIV infection, when a person's immune system is severely damaged and has difficulty fighting diseases and certain cancers. Prior to the development of certain medications, people with HIV could progress to AIDS in just a few years. But now, people can live much longer, even decades, before they develop AIDS.

How Is HIV Spread?

HIV is transmitted through an infected person's body fluids. This includes:

- Blood

- Semen

- Vaginal secretions

- Breast milk

- Other body fluids or OPIM if blood is present

Although HIV can sometimes be detected in saliva, tears, urine, cerebrospinal fluid and amniotic fluid, exposure to these fluids from an infected person does not result in transmission of the virus. The greatest risk for health care workers involves exposure to the more than

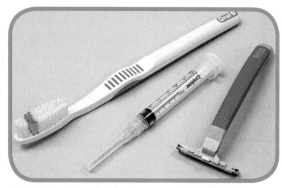

Figure 2-7 *Hepatitis may be transmitted by blood on any personal item.*

1 million HIV-positive people in the United States, 21% of whom are unaware of their infection. Additionally, an estimated 56,300 Americans become infected with HIV each year. Health care workers often come in contact with these carriers when they seek medical care for other health issues.

Some health care workers have been infected with HIV through work-related exposures involving blood or other infected substances **(Figure 2-8).** Infection is most likely to occur with exposure to HIV-contaminated blood, blood components or blood products through:

- Injection through the skin
- Unprotected mucous membranes
- An open skin wound

Casual contact with those infected with HIV does not result in transmission of the virus.

Casual contact includes such things as the following:

- Sharing food, utensils or a drinking glass
- Kissing, hugging or touching
- Being around someone who sneezes or coughs
- Sharing a phone or bathroom

HIV is not an airborne virus, nor can it be contracted from the bite of a mosquito, flea, tick or other bloodsucking vermin.

Symptoms of HIV

Within a few weeks of being infected with HIV, some people develop flu-like symptoms that last for a week or two. Many people with HIV have no symptoms and do not even know they have been infected. People living with HIV may appear and feel healthy for several years, but HIV is still affecting their bodies.

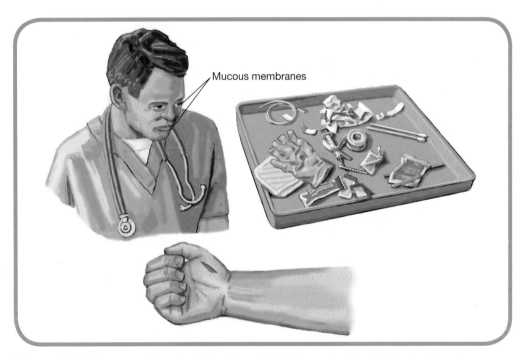

Mucous membranes

Figure 2-8 *In occupational exposures, HIV can enter the body in 3 main ways: through mucous membranes such as in the mouth or eyes, by unintentional injection into the body or by entry through any cut or non-intact area of skin.*

Late-stage HIV (AIDS) symptoms may include the following:

- Poor appetite
- Rapid weight loss
- Fever
- Skin rashes
- Swollen lymph nodes
- Diarrhea
- Tiredness
- Night sweats
- An inability to fight off infection

How Do I Know If I Have HIV?

The only reliable way to determine if a person has HIV is through a blood test. The most commonly used HIV tests detect HIV antibodies, the substances the body creates in response to becoming infected with HIV. Most people will develop detectable antibodies within 2-8 weeks of their infection. Ninety-seven percent of persons will develop detectable antibodies in the first 3 months. Therefore, a person should consider a follow-up test more than 3 months after their last potential exposure to HIV. In extremely rare cases, it can take up to 6 months to develop antibodies to HIV.

Rapid HIV tests also are available that can give results in as little as 20 minutes. A positive HIV test result means a person may be infected with HIV. All positive HIV test results from either rapid or conventional testing must be verified by a second, confirmation HIV test.

Prevention of HIV Infection

No vaccine is currently available for HIV, and there is no cure for HIV/AIDS. Therefore, preventive measures are very important. Safe work practice controls significantly reduce the risk of contracting HIV in the workplace or transmitting infectious diseases to victims. These guidelines include the following:

- Regular hand washing
- Use of barriers
- Universal precautions

Lesson 3 discusses these guidelines in detail. Compared with HBV, HIV does not live long outside the human body and is easily killed with disinfectants.

Learning Checkpoint 4

1. True or False: All people develop HIV symptoms 3 months after exposure.

2. True or False: About 20% of all HIV-positive people do not know they have the infection.

3. True or False: HIV can enter the body only through broken skin.

4. True or False: HIV can be contracted by sharing a fork with an infectious person.

5. What are the most common symptoms of late-stage HIV (AIDS)? (Check all that apply.)

_____ a. Frequent sneezing		_____ e. Swollen lymph nodes	
_____ b. Rapid weight loss		_____ f. Red spots under fingernails	
_____ c. Heart attack		_____ g. Skin rashes	
_____ d. Fever		_____ h. Fatigue	

6. True or False: HIV infection can be prevented in health care settings.

Select Other Diseases Caused by Bloodborne Pathogens

Disease	Pathogen	Mode of Transmission	Common Signs and Symptoms	Prevention	Treatment
Hepatitis A Short-term (not chronic) infection becoming less common with widely used vaccine in the United States	Hepatitis A virus (HAV)	Primarily by fecal-oral route, usually fecally contaminated food or water Anal sex Exposure to blood or OPIM (rare)	Jaundice, fatigue, abdominal pain, loss of appetite, nausea, diarrhea, fever A very small percentage of patients have more serious complications.	Hand washing and good hygiene Vaccination Short-term protection from immune globulin after exposure	No specific treatment 99% of patients fully recover
Hepatitis E Usually occurs in outbreaks in areas with inadequate environmental sanitation; most cases in U.S. result from travel elsewhere. Does not cause chronic liver disease.	Hepatitis E virus (HEV)	Primarily by fecal-oral route, usually fecally contaminated drinking water Person-to-person transmission (rare)	Abdominal pain, loss of appetite, dark urine, fever, jaundice, malaise, nausea and vomiting	Use of clean water supply; avoiding uncooked shellfish, fruits and vegetables No vaccine available	No specific treatment Almost all patients fully recover
Syphilis Over 32,000 cases in United States in 2002	Treponema pallidum bacterium	Vaginal, anal or oral sex Mother to fetus	Primary stage: Sore (chancre) on external genitals, vagina, anus or rectum or lips and mouth Secondary stage: Rashes, fever, swollen lymph glands, sore throat, aches, fatigue Late Stage: Internal damage causing uncoordinated movement, paralysis, blindness, dementia	Abstinence from sexual contact Correct and consistent use of latex condoms reduces the risk of transmission	Easily cured with antibiotics in early stages Treatment in late stages less effective

Disease	Pathogen	Mode of Transmission	Common Signs and Symptoms	Prevention	Treatment
Ebola Hemorrhagic Fever Has occurred since 1976 in sporadic outbreaks in Africa. Has not appeared in the United States.	Ebola virus	First transmission at the start of an outbreak is unknown (may be contact with infected animal) Transmitted among humans by contact with infected person's blood or OPIM	Fever, headache, joint and muscle aches, sore throat, weakness; followed by diarrhea, vomiting, stomach pain. Some infected people may have rash, red eyes and internal and external bleeding.	During an outbreak: isolation of Ebola patients and use of barrier devices and all bloodborne pathogen infection control guidelines	Supportive care only; no cure. Still unknown why some patients recover while others die.
Malaria Common in over 100 countries; more than 40% of the world population is at risk. 300-500 million cases occur yearly (World Health Organization). A few cases occur annually in the United States	4 different Plasmodium species (parasites)	The bite of a malaria-infected mosquito Blood transfusions Mother to fetus	Fever, flu-like symptoms (shaking chills, headache, muscle aches, fatigue, nausea and vomiting, diarrhea, anemia, jaundice) One type may cause kidney failure, seizures, coma, death	Vaccination and anti-malarial drugs Prevention of mosquito bites	Generally can be cured with prescription drugs, type and length of treatment depending on type of malaria and other factors
West Nile Virus Seasonal epidemic in North America	West Nile virus	Usually by bite of infected mosquito Blood transfusions (rare) Mother to fetus or to infant through breast milk (rare)	No symptoms in 80% of infected people Mild symptoms in 20%: fever, headache, body aches, nausea and vomiting, swollen lymph glands, rash Serious symptoms in 1 in 150 people: high fever, neck stiffness, stupor, coma, tremors, convulsions, vision loss, paralysis	Prevention of mosquito bites Elimination of mosquito breeding sites	No specific treatment Supportive care for severe cases

Source: Centers for Disease Control and Prevention.

2 • Bloodborne Pathogens

Lesson 3 • Preventing Infection from Bloodborne Pathogens

Lesson Preview

- Engineering Controls
- Work Practice Controls
- Personal Protective Equipment
- Universal Precautions

- Emergency Procedures for Unexpected Exposure
- Exposure Control Plans

The OSHA Occupational Exposure to Bloodborne Pathogens Standard (the Standard) requires employers to use 4 types of strategies to reduce occupational exposure to bloodborne pathogens:

1. Engineering controls

2. Work practice controls

3. Personal protective equipment

4. Universal precautions

In addition, the Standard requires having procedures in place in the event an exposure does occur and maintaining an Exposure Control Plan.

Engineering Controls

OSHA defines **engineering controls** as devices that isolate or remove the bloodborne pathogen hazard from the workplace. Many kinds of devices have been developed to increase safety in the workplace. These devices include needleless IV systems, self-sheathing needles or syringes, eye wash stations, hand washing facilities, sharps containers and biohazard labels. These all have an important role in reducing the risk of exposure to bloodborne pathogens.

Sharps

Sharp is a general term for any device or item that may accidentally penetrate the skin of a person handling it. Examples of sharps are needles, scissors, scalpels, disposable razors used for shaving in nursing homes, health care and correctional facilities, and broken glassware **(Figure 3-1)**.

Hollow bore needles pose one of the greatest risks to health care workers. Safer needleless systems are now used in many settings for

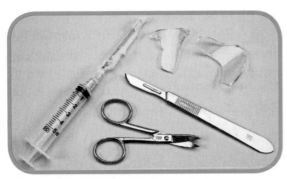

Figure 3-1 *Different types of sharps.*

administering medications. Other systems have needle shields, retractable needles or other protective devices. Employers are not necessarily required to use the latest devices but must evaluate the feasibility of such devices annually **(Figure 3-2).** Employers must document which commercially available engineering controls are being considered and whether they will be implemented. OSHA requires employers to include input from non-managerial employees in the selection process.

Approved sharps containers must be available in appropriate places for safe disposal of used sharps. These containers must be leak proof, resistant to puncture and other damage, able to be securely closed, upright and labeled with a biohazard warning **(Figure 3-3).** Sharps

containers must be replaced routinely so they do not overfill. The containers for reusable sharps such as scissors are not required to be closable, as these containers likely will be reused.

Hand Washing Facilities and Eye Wash Stations

When possible, hand washing facilities must be provided for all employees. When not possible, alcohol-based hand rubs may be provided instead. Eye wash stations should be available when appropriate for flushing contaminants from the eyes **(Figure 3-4).**

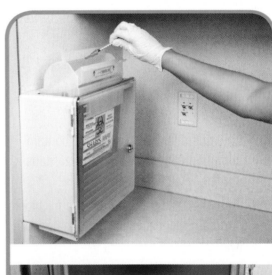

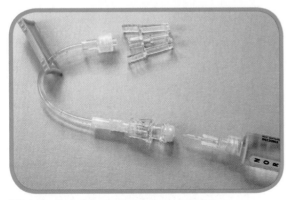

Figure 3-2 *New devices provide safeguards against an unintentional needlestick.*

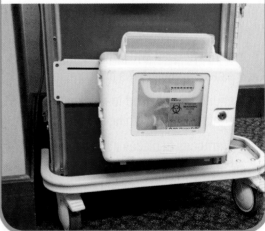

Figure 3-3 *Wall-mounted and cart-mounted sharps containers.*

Figure 3-4 *An eye wash station is used to flush a substance that has splashed in the eyes.*

Warning Labels

Warning labels are required to be prominently displayed on the following:

- Containers for waste that may contain contaminated materials (biohazardous waste)
- Freezers and refrigerators used for blood or other potentially infectious materials (OPIM)
- Containers used to transport, ship or store blood or OPIM
- Contaminated equipment until proper cleaning procedures are complete
- Laundry bags used to hold and transport contaminated clothing
- Entrances to places containing potentially infectious materials

All potentially infectious waste must be disposed of in properly labeled red containers or in containers clearly marked with a red, orange or orange-red label with the universal biohazard symbol **(Figure 3-5)**.

ALERT!
ANTISEPTIC HAND CLEANSER

If antiseptic towelettes or antibacterial hand washing liquid is used without water for the initial cleaning after an exposure, a thorough scrubbing with soap and water is still needed as soon as possible.

Work Practice Controls

Work practice controls are controls that reduce the likelihood of exposure by altering the manner in which a task is performed. Depending upon the environment, work practice controls might include using personal protective equipment (PPE), hand washing, decontaminating and sterilizing equipment and areas, safely handling sharps, correctly disposing of wastes, safely handling laundry and good personal habits **(Figure 3-6)**.

Hand Hygiene

Hand hygiene means performing hand washing or using antiseptic hand wash or alcohol-based hand rubs. Hand hygiene is important because bacteria can survive for days on equipment and other surfaces (e.g., bed rails, IV pumps,

Figure 3-5 *The universal biohazard symbol.*

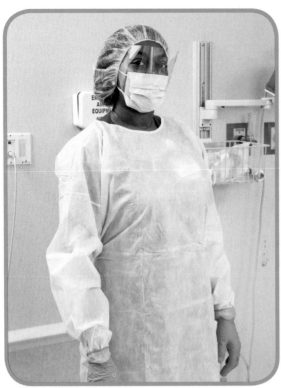

Figure 3-6 *Safe work practice controls include use of personal protective equipment.*

computer keyboards). It is a simple but very important step for preventing the transmission of bloodborne pathogens.

Hand Washing

The following are general guidelines to use with hand washing:

- Wash any exposed skin, ideally with antibacterial soap, as soon after an exposure as possible.

- While washing, be gentle with any scabs or sores.

- Wash all surfaces, including the backs of hands, wrists, between the fingers and under fingernails.

- Wash hands immediately after removing gloves or other PPE.

Antiseptic towelettes and waterless antibacterial hand washing liquid can be used when soap and running water are not available. If one of these methods is used for the initial cleaning after a potential exposure, however, a thorough scrubbing with soap and water is still recommended as soon as possible and is required if there was exposure to blood or OPIM.

Alcohol-Based Hand Rubs

Use of alcohol-based hand rubs is the preferred method of hand hygiene in health care settings in all situations except when hands are visibly dirty or contaminated. Hand rubs are encouraged in health care settings because they require less time to use and are more accessible than sinks. Other benefits of hand rubs include their ability to reduce bacterial counts on hands more than soap and water alone and are less drying and irritating to the skin than soap and water **(Figure 3-7).**

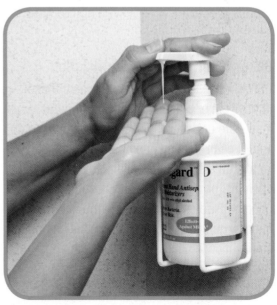

Figure 3-7 *Alcohol-based hand rubs reduce bacterial counts on hands.*

Learning Checkpoint 1

1. True or False: Sharps include scissors, disposable razors used for shaving in nursing homes and needles.

2. Engineering controls include: (Check all that apply.)

   _____ a. Needleless injection systems

   _____ b. Eye wash stations

   _____ c. Biohazard labels

3. True or False: Employers are required to purchase all newly developed devices that help prevent employees from exposure to bloodborne pathogens.

4. Name at least 3 places biohazardous warning labels must appear:

   _____

 **ALERT!**
HAND WASHING

Before handling any potentially infectious materials, know where the nearest hand washing facility is. You can use facilities such as restrooms, janitor closets and laboratory sinks, as long as soap is available. Do not use sinks in areas where food is prepared. Merely wetting the hands will not prevent infection.

Decontamination and Sterilization

OSHA defines **decontamination** as the use of physical or chemical means to remove, inactivate or destroy bloodborne pathogens on a surface or item so it is no longer infectious. To **sterilize** something means to use a chemical or physical procedure to destroy all microbial life on the item. Use the following general guidelines for decontamination and sterilization:

- All reusable sharps, such as knives, scissors and scalpels, must be cleaned and sterilized after being used:

  – Before cleaning, store sharps in a container with a wide opening.

  – Use forceps or tongs to remove contaminated sharps from containers.

- Decontaminate equipment and working surfaces, bench tops and floors with an approved commercial disinfectant or a 10% bleach solution:

  – At the end of a work shift

  – As surfaces become obviously contaminated

  – After any spill of blood or OPIM

- Disinfect personal items, such as jewelry and nail brushes, after hand washing.

- Use utensils, such as tongs or a dustpan, to clean up broken glass and other contaminated materials for disposal in a sharps container.

1 Wet hands with water.

2 Apply enough soap to cover all hand surfaces.

3 Rub hands palm to palm.

4 Rub right palm over left, with interlaced fingers and vice versa.

5 Rub palm to palm with fingers interlaced.

6 Rub backs of fingers to opposing palms with fingers interlocked.

7 Rub left thumb clasped in right palm and vise versa.

8 Rotational rubbing, backwards and forwards with clasped fingers of right hand in left palm and vice versa.

9 Rinse hands with water.

10 Dry hands thoroughly with paper towel and dispose of properly.

11 Use towel to turn off faucet and open door.

This procedure should take 40-60 seconds.

3 • Preventing Infection from Bloodborne Pathogens

Skill — Cleaning Broken Sharps and a Contaminated Spill

1 Wear heavy utility gloves and other personal protective equipment to protect yourself while cleaning the spill.

2 Bring supplies and hazardous waste containers to the location of the spill.

3 Use tongs or other means to pick up any broken glass, and dispose of it in an appropriate sharps container.

4 Absorb the entire spill with paper towels and dispose of them in the biohazard container before using disinfectant.

5 Disinfect the area thoroughly with an approved disinfectant.

6 Remove your gloves and wash your hands.

☣ ALERT!
PICKING UP SHARPS OR BROKEN GLASS

The Standard states that employees should never pick up broken glass or other sharps with gloved or bare hands. Always use tongs or some other device to pick them up. Do not use a vacuum cleaner. Never touch broken glass with your hands. Have all supplies ready before starting cleanup.

Using a Commercial Body Fluid Disposal Kit

1 Wearing disposable apron, eye shield/ face mask, shoe covers and medical exam gloves, sprinkle absorbent over the blood spill until fluid is absorbed completely.

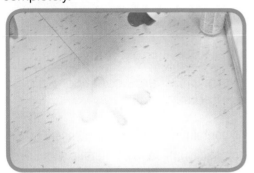

2 Use a scoop and scraper to scrape up the absorbent material. Discard the material scoop and scraper in red biohazard bag.

3 Spray disinfectant/cleaner over the spill area. Allow it to remain wet for about 10 minutes. Use paper towels to wipe up the disinfectant. Discard paper towels in red biohazard bag.

4 Discard apron, eye shield/face mask, shoe covers and medical exam gloves in red biohazard bag and dispose of the bag according to federal, state and local regulations. Wash hands thoroughly with soap and water.

Handling Sharps

Guidelines for safe handling of sharps include the following:

- Employers must put sharps disposal containers in easily accessible areas where sharps are used **(Figure 3-8).**

- Needles must not be recapped, removed, bent, sheared or broken.

- The entire needle/syringe assembly must be disposed of in a sharps container.

- Only when medically necessary, a mechanical device may be used to recap a contaminated needle or remove it from a disposable syringe. OSHA requires that the exposure control plan must specify when, why and how this is done and by whom.

Regulated Waste Handling and Disposal

The Standard has provisions to protect employees during the containment, storage and transport of regulated waste other than contaminated sharps. However, OSHA does not regulate the final disposal of regulated waste. According to OSHA, the final disposal of regulated waste must be in accordance with applicable regulations of the United States, states and territories, and political subdivisions of states and territories.

Regulated waste includes:

- Blood or OPIM in liquid or semi-liquid state

- Items contaminated with blood or OPIM that could release liquid or semi-liquid blood or OPIM if squeezed

- Items with dried blood that could be spread by handling

- Contaminated sharps

- Lab specimens containing blood or OPIM

Figure 3-8 *Sharps container inside an ambulance.*

All containers intended for disposal of potentially infectious materials should be clearly marked with the universal biohazard symbol **(Figure 3-5).** The facility must follow approved procedures for disposing of regulated waste and disinfecting equipment for reuse.

Laundry

Uniforms, clothing and cloth supplies should be kept free from contamination when possible. Clothing intended to prevent contact with blood that becomes contaminated with blood or OPIM must be put in special laundry bags that are clearly labeled and color-coded to be sent to an approved laundry facility for cleaning. OSHA has stated that, "home laundering is unacceptable because the employer cannot ensure that proper handling or laundering procedures are being followed and because contamination could migrate to the homes of employees."[1]

Employers are responsible for cleaning, laundering and/or disposing of personal protective equipment. The CDC in the "2003 Guidelines for Environmental Infection Control in Health-Care Facilities" provides guidance for the handling, cleaning and disinfection of contaminated laundry.

[1](CPL 02-02-069 XIII.D.16 Accessed 9/22/11)

Many agencies use yellow bags with the biohazard symbol affixed to them to avoid confusion with red bags, which usually contain materials for disposal **(Figure 3-9).** Anyone handling contaminated laundry must be trained to handle bloodborne pathogens and must wear appropriate PPE.

⚠ ALERT!
CONTAMINATED CLOTHING

Never take contaminated clothing home to wash. Keep extra clothing at work in case your street clothes become contaminated and must be sent to the approved laundry facility.

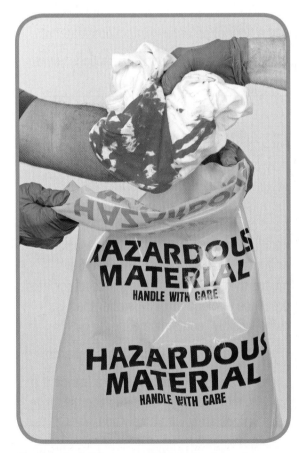

Figure 3-9 *Biohazard laundry bag for contaminated clothing.*

Work Area Restrictions

When working in an area where bloodborne pathogen exposure may occur, prevent entry of pathogens into your mouth or eyes by keeping your hands away from your face. In general, follow these guidelines:

- Do not smoke.
- Do not put on lip balm, hand lotion or cosmetics.
- Do not eat or drink.
- Do not handle your contact lenses.
- Do not store food or beverages in places where blood is stored or handled, including in refrigerators, freezers, shelves or cabinets or on countertops or bench tops where blood or OPIM are present.
- Do not put pencils, pens or other objects in your mouth where potentially infectious materials may be present.
- Do not use a sink that is used for food preparation for any other cleanup.

Personal Protective Equipment

Personal protective equipment consists of barriers such as gloves, jumpsuits or aprons, eye shields or goggles, face masks or face shields and caps and booties you wear to protect yourself from exposure to blood and OPIM. The Standard requires your employer to provide you with appropriate PPE at no cost to you. Your employer also must train you in how to use this equipment and must clean, repair or replace it as needed.

In any situation where exposure to bloodborne pathogens is a possibility, wear your PPE.

Learning Checkpoint 2

1. True or False: If you wash your hands with waterless soap, further cleansing is not necessary.

2. True or False: Equipment must be decontaminated with a 25% bleach solution.

3. Regulated waste includes: (Check all that apply.)

   _____ a. Contaminated sharps

   _____ b. Clothing with dried blood on it

   _____ c. Lab specimens containing OPIM

   _____ d. Dressings and bandages that could release blood if squeezed

4. True or False: Eating in an area used for lab research on human tissue specimens poses little risk and is generally acceptable as long as you wear gloves.

5. When should you always clean under your fingernails when washing your hands?

   _____

6. True or False: Never use a vacuum cleaner to clean a floor of potentially infectious material.

7. Describe what to do if your clothing briefly contacts a spill that may contain an infectious liquid.

   _____

Gloves

Gloves are a type of barrier which, like other barriers, separate you from potentially infectious materials **(Figure 3-10)**. Medical exam gloves suitable for protection from bloodborne pathogens are made of nitrile, vinyl, latex or other waterproof materials.

Figure 3-10 *Wear gloves whenever you may contact blood or OPIM.*

For added barrier protection, 2 pairs of gloves may be worn together in some situations. At a minimum, gloves must be used where there is reasonable anticipation of employee hand contact with blood or OPIM and when handling or touching contaminated surfaces or items. Here, the term "contaminated" means the presence or reasonable anticipated presence of blood or OPIM, rather than just being "visibly" contaminated.

When using gloves, you must remember to:

- **Check that your gloves are intact.** If a hole or tear is present, replace the glove immediately with a new one.

- **Not use petroleum-based hand lotions.** These lotions may cause latex gloves to disintegrate.

Skill: Putting on Gloves

1 Pull glove onto 1 hand.

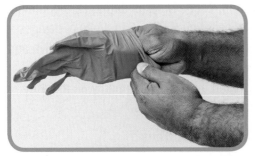

2 Pull glove tight.

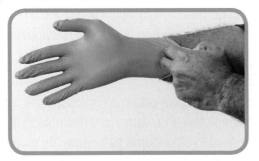

3 Put on other glove.

- **Remove contaminated gloves carefully.** Do not touch any part of the contaminated material on the outside of the gloves.

- **Dispose of gloves properly.** After working with any material that may be infected by bloodborne pathogens, dispose of your gloves in a container clearly marked for biohazardous waste.

ALERT!
LATEX ALLERGY

People who frequently wear latex gloves have a potential risk of developing a latex allergy. This reaction may include a skin rash or even cause difficulty breathing. If you experience signs of an allergy when wearing gloves, ask your employer for latex-free or hypoallergenic gloves made of nitrile or vinyl.

Protective Body Clothing

Jumpsuits, aprons, lab coats and gowns are sometimes worn to protect clothing from contamination by blood and OPIM. These barriers are available in different thicknesses and materials. Any articles of clothing that become contaminated with blood should be removed immediately and handled as carefully as any contaminated item. Avoid contact with your skin, and put the article in a clearly marked biohazardous laundry bag.

Goggles and Eye Shields

Certain occupations or work conditions involve a risk of being splashed in the face by blood or substances contaminated with bloodborne pathogens. Because the eyes are surrounded by mucous membranes, a splash in the eyes may allow bloodborne pathogens into the body. Use of barrier devices is therefore often essential. Eye protection is also recommended when cleaning spills or performing first aid.

PPE for the eyes includes goggles and safety glasses with side shields. Face shields also protect the eyes **(Figure 3-11).** If you are wearing prescription eyeglasses, you must use side shields. Both the glasses and the side shields must be decontaminated according to the schedule set by your employer.

Face Shields and Face Masks

Face shields protect the eyes, mouth and nose from splashes and contaminants. Face masks protect the mouth and nose. When worn with

goggles or safety glasses, face masks help protect the whole face **(Figure 3-12).** Pocket face masks and face shields are used when giving rescue breaths during cardiopulmonary resuscitation (CPR). Both types of devices offer protection from the victim's saliva and other fluids, as well as from the victim's exhaled air when equipped with a 1-way valve **(Figure 3-13).**

Caps and Booties

The forehead and the hair may be covered by a waterproof disposable cap, and shoes or boots by waterproof, disposable booties. Both provide additional barriers to bloodborne pathogens.

Improvising Personal Protective Equipment

In unexpected or extreme circumstances, you may not have PPE with you when potentially exposed to bloodborne pathogens. Be creative in using items at hand to avoid contact with potentially infectious material. Using a plastic bag, a sheet or a towel or even removing an article of clothing to use as a barrier is better than being unprotected **(Figure 3-14).** Dispose of or decontaminate any articles you use as barriers as you would any contaminated item.

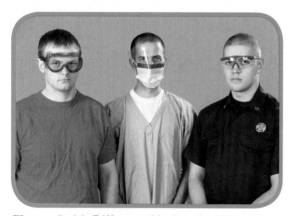

Figure 3-11 *Different kinds of eye protection are available.*

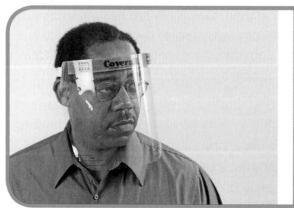
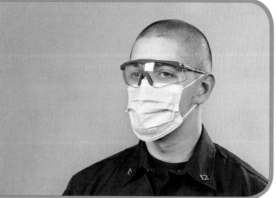

Figure 3-12 *Different kinds of face protection are available.*

Figure 3-13 *Pocket face masks and face shields are used during CPR.*

Disposing of Contaminated Personal Protective Equipment

Different forms of protective equipment require different disposal methods. Your employer may request that you put articles such as used gloves in a designated container for storage until they are disposed of. Contaminated clothing may be stored in clearly labeled bags until it is decontaminated, laundered or properly disposed of.

Universal Precautions

Universal precautions is a phrase describing safety guidelines in which all blood and OPIM are handled as if they are contaminated. When universal precautions are followed, it does not matter whether you know the source of the substance. Under universal precautions, you treat all materials as if they are infected with bloodborne pathogens. This includes the following:

- Blood
- Semen
- Vaginal secretions
- Saliva that may contain blood
- Cerebrospinal fluid

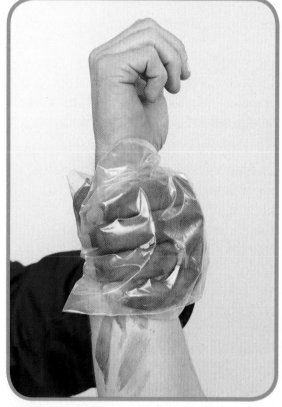

Figure 3-14 *Always use a barrier – improvise when necessary.*

- Synovial fluid
- Pleural fluid
- Any body fluid where blood is visible
- Any body fluid that cannot be identified

Following universal precautions means using PPE and following all the safe work practice controls described in this workbook.

Body Substance Isolation

Body substance isolation (BSI) is an alternative approach to universal precautions. BSI guidelines define all body fluids and substances as infectious. Since OSHA now requires all body fluids to be managed with universal precautions, this approach is essentially the same as BSI.

UNIVERSAL PRECAUTIONS AND ALL BODY FLUIDS

Previously, universal precautions did not apply to other body fluids, such as nasal secretions, sweat, tears and urine and feces, which were not considered potentially infectious.

Currently, however, an OSHA written interpretation states universal precautions should apply to all body fluids because it is impossible to know by looking whether these other body fluids may contain traces of blood. Therefore, assume all body fluids may be infectious and always follow universal precautions.

REQUIRED INFORMATION WHEN REPORTING EXPOSURE INCIDENTS

- Date and time of your exposure
- Your job title/classification
- Your work location where the exposure happened
- Activity you were performing at the time of the exposure
- Your training for that activity
- Engineering controls (devices and equipment) you were using at the time of the exposure
- Preventive work practice controls you were using at the time of the exposure
- Personal protective equipment you were using at the time of the exposure

Standard Precautions

The health care industry uses the term standard precautions to describe the guidelines for handling blood and OPIM. According to the CDC, standard precautions combine the major features of universal precautions and body substance isolation and are based on the principle that all blood, body fluids, secretions, excretions except sweat, non-in-contact skin and mucous membranes may contain transmissible infectious agents.[2]

Standard precautions include a group of infection prevention practices that apply to all patients, regardless of suspected or confirmed infection status, in any setting in which health care is delivered. They include hand hygiene, use of gloves, gown, mask, eye protection or face shield, depending on the anticipated exposure, and safe injection practices. Standard precautions are considered more stringent than universal precautions alone.

Emergency Procedures for an Unexpected Exposure Incident

Even when you follow all safety guidelines and universal precautions, an unexpected exposure can occur. If so, both you and your employer need to take immediate action. Employers are required to inform you how to make an incident report in case you are exposed. A sample exposure incident report form can be found on pages 49-50.

If you are exposed take the following actions:

- If blood or OPIM splashes in your eyes or other mucous membranes, flush the area with running water for 20 minutes if possible.

(continues on page 36)

[2](The Centers for Disease Control and Prevention, Guideline for Isolation Precautions: "Preventing Transmission of Infectious Agents in Healthcare Settings 2007," p. 66)

1 With your gloved dominant hand, grasp the other glove at the wrist or palm and pull it away from the hand.

2 Pull the glove the rest of the way off.

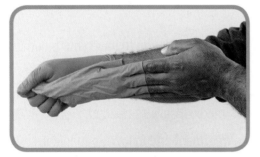

3 Holding the removed glove balled up in the palm of your gloved hand, insert fingers of your non-dominant hand under the cuff of the remaining glove.

4 Remove the glove by stretching it up and away from the hand turning it inside out as you pull it off.

5 Dispose of gloves in a biohazard container, and wash your hands.

3 • Preventing Infection from Bloodborne Pathogens

Learning Checkpoint 3

1. True or False: Mucous membranes of the face can be protected by wearing a mask and goggles.

2. Check off items below considered personal protective equipment:

_____ a. Latex gloves   _____ d. Booties

_____ b. Face shield   _____ e. Jumpsuit

_____ c. Face mask   _____ f. Goggles

3. True or False: It is acceptable to patch a small hole in your gloves with a Band-Aid.

4. True or False: Used gloves should be disposed of like hazardous waste.

5. True or False: Your employer should arrange for you to purchase your necessary personal protective equipment at an employee discount.

(continued from page 34)

- Wash any exposed area well with soap, using an antibacterial soap if possible.

- Treat any scabs and sores gently when cleaning your skin.

- Report the exposure to your supervisor as soon as possible on the day the exposure occurrs to assure prompt evaluation.

- Save any potentially contaminated object for testing purposes.

- Seek medical care as soon as possible.

After receiving your report, your employer must do the following:

- Identify and document the person or other source of the blood or OPIM.

- Obtain consent to test the source person's blood and arrange for testing the person (unless he or she is already known to be infectious). If the source refuses testing or if the source is unknown, the employee is stil offered evaluation.

- Inform you of the test results.

- Arrange for you to have your blood tested if you consent.

- Arrange for you to receive counseling and medical care as needed.

The treatment and follow-up medical care depends on the type of exposure: the substance involved, the route of transmission and the severity of the exposure. Treatment may include a hepatitis B vaccination or treatment with hepatitis B immune globulin.

Figure 3-15 *After an exposure your employer will work with you to arrange any needed testing and treatment.*

Figure 3-16 *Employees have the right to see the Exposure Control Plan.*

An **exposure incident report form** is kept in the employee's confidential file **(Figure 3-15).** By federal law, employers must maintain strict confidentiality about any exposure incident.

 **ALERT!**
EXPOSURE INCIDENT

Don't delay acting if you are exposed to blood or OPIM. Every minute counts in preventing pathogens from entering the body.

Exposure Control Plans

OSHA requires employers to have an **Exposure Control Plan** to prevent exposure to bloodborne pathogens. Your employer's Exposure Control Plan should do the following:

- Identify the job positions and individuals to receive training.
- Establish necessary engineering controls and work practice controls.
- Specify PPE to be used.
- Require using universal precautions.
- State the opportunity for a hepatitis B vaccination.
- Include other measures appropriate for your specific work environment.

The Exposure Control Plan must be reviewed and updated at least annually and whenever necessary to reflect any changes in work practice controls related to possible exposure to bloodborne pathogens. The plan should also describe how improved safety devices are to be evaluated for possible use. It is essential that employees who are covered under the Exposure Control Plan be trained according to the plan. These employees also must have access to the plan.

The Standard requires that employers inform new employees about their plan and conduct training before performing any work tasks that would put you at risk for an exposure. Refresher training is required annually or whenever changes are made to policies and procedures **(Figure 3-16).**

A sample exposure control plan can be found on pages 53-57.

Learning Checkpoint 4

1. True or False: Universal precautions need to be followed only when there is a risk of exposure to a known bloodborne pathogen.

2. True or False: If blood or OPIM is splashed in your eye, flush the area for 3-5 minutes.

3. True or False: If an exposure incident occurs, it is important to identify the source of the blood or OPIM.

4. What information must you report to your employer if you have been exposed to a bloodborne pathogen? (Check all that apply.)

   _____ a. PPE you were using

   _____ b. Time and date of exposure

   _____ c. What you were doing at the time

   _____ d. Work practice controls being used

   _____ e. Location of incident

   _____ f. Engineering controls in use

5. When you report an exposure incident, your employer should – (Check all that apply.)

   _____ a. obtain the source individual's consent for testing.

   _____ b. inform you of the source individual's test results.

   _____ c. arrange for you to have your blood tested.

   _____ d. arrange for you to receive counseling and medical care as needed.

6. When do you as an employee have the right to see your employer's Exposure Control Plan?

   _____

   _____

Lesson 4 • Airborne Pathogens

Lesson Preview

- Types of Airborne Pathogens
- Tuberculosis
- Influenza

OSHA regulations do not currently specify specific employee protections from airborne pathogens in the same manner as the Occupational Exposure to Bloodborne Pathogens Standard specifies protections against bloodborne pathogens. OSHA does expect employers to protect employees from known hazards, however, which in certain settings can include airborne pathogens such as tuberculosis (TB). OSHA enforces this protection for workers through the Occupational Safety and Health Act of 1970 or the General Duty Clause (Public Law 91-596). A new OSHA standard for tuberculosis has been proposed but has yet to be implemented. The information in this lesson is based on the 2005 CDC guidelines for preventing transmission of tuberculosis in health care settings and on CDC's general information on influenza.

What Are Airborne Pathogens?

Airborne pathogens are disease-causing microorganisms spread from person to person in the form of droplet nuclei in the air. There are three types of airborne pathogens:

- Viral
- Bacterial
- Fungal

Meningitis, influenza, pneumonia and TB are examples of diseases transmitted through the air. This Lesson focuses on TB because that is a common airborne disease for which employees may be at risk. Influenza is also included in the Lesson because it is a common airborne pathogen. Many of the precautions taken to prevent TB will also lower the risk of infection from other airborne pathogens such as influenza.

Airborne pathogens differ from bloodborne pathogens in that they are spread by inhalation of the germ. An infectious person's coughing, sneezing, laughing or singing can send tiny droplets of moisture into the air that contain the pathogen. Depending on the environment, these contaminants can remain airborne for several hours.

Although an airborne pathogen may be transmitted if the pathogen is inhaled, exposure to airborne pathogens does not always result in infection. The likelihood of infection depends on the following:

- How contagious the infectious person is
- Where the exposure occurs
- How long the exposure lasts
- How healthy you are at the time of the exposure

Tuberculosis

TB disease was once the leading cause of death in the United States. Starting in the 1940s, scientists discovered the first of several medicines used to treat TB and, as a result, TB slowly began to decrease in the United States. However, in the 1970s and early 1980s, TB control efforts were neglected. As a result, between 1985 and 1992 the number of TB cases increased. With increased attention to the TB problem, the number of persons with TB has been declining steadily since 1992. In 2010, TB rates decreased to 3.6 cases per 100,000 population. This is the lowest rate reported since national TB surveillance began in the United States in 1953. But TB is still a problem; 11,181 cases were reported in 2010 in the United States.[1]

Tuberculosis is caused by a specific bacteria, Mycobacterium **(Figure 4-1)**. The disease usually affects the lungs, but it can also affect the brain, spine, lymph nodes or kidneys. Many people with a **TB infection** may not be sick because their bodies are effectively fighting the bacteria; these people are not contagious. Later, however, they may develop **TB disease** and become contagious. About 5-10% of people with a TB infection develop the disease sometime during their lifetime. The risk is higher for people with certain medical conditions such as:

[1](www.cdc.gov/mmwr/preview/mmwrhtml/ mm6011a3.htm?s_cid=mm6011a3_e%0D%0A Accessed 9/21/2011)

- HIV
- Diabetes mellitus
- Severe kidney disease
- Low body weight
- Certain types of cancer (leukemia, Hodgkin's disease, or cancer of the head and neck)

HIV infection is the most important known risk factor for progression from latent TB infection to TB disease. Progression to TB disease is often rapid among HIV-infected people and can be deadly. In addition, TB outbreaks can rapidly expand in HIV-infected patient groups. There are a number of treatment options for HIV-infected people with either latent TB infection or active TB disease. State and local health departments should be consulted about these treatment options.

According to the CDC, employees in certain workplaces also face a greater risk of exposure. These workplaces include but are not limited to the following:

- Correctional facilities
- Drug and treatment centers
- Health care facilities (emergency departments, patient rooms, medical offices and clinics, home-based health care, Emergency Medical Services)

Figure 4-1 *The bacteria that causes tuberculosis.*

- Homeless shelters
- Long-term care facilities
- Morgues

How Is TB Spread?

TB is spread when a person inhales the TB pathogen, which may be present in the air after an infected person coughs or sneezes. Depending on room size, ventilation and other factors, the TB pathogen can live in the air and on contaminated objects for a few hours, especially in small places with no fresh air. Once inhaled, M. tuberculosis bacteria travel to lung alveoli and establish infection. About 2-12 weeks after infection, the person's immune response limits activity, and the infection is detectable. Some bacteria survive and lay dormant for years (latent TB infection, or LTBI).

Symptoms of TB

People with TB infection often have no symptoms and do not feel sick. If the infection advances to TB disease, however, the person's symptoms may include:

- Weight loss
- Fever
- Night sweats
- Weakness

If the TB affects the person's lungs, the common symptoms include a bad cough that lasts 3 weeks or longer, production of sputum, chest pain and coughing up blood. Other symptoms depend on the part of the body affected **(Figure 4-2)**.

How Do I Know If I Have TB?

The **tuberculin skin test (TST),** also called the **Mantoux test,** reveals whether a person is infected with the TB bacteria. This test is performed by injecting a small amount of tuberculin fluid under the skin in the lower part of the arm. The test spot result is checked 2-3 days later by a health care worker.

TB blood tests measure how the immune system reacts to the bacteria that cause TB. Only one visit is required to draw blood for the test.

QuantiFERON–TB GOLD In-Tube test (GFT-GIT) and T-SPOT TB test are two Food and Drug Administration approved TB blood tests. Test results generally are available in 24-48 hours.

A person with latent TB infection:	A person with active TB disease:
Usually has a skin test or blood test indicating TB infection.	Usually has a skin test or blood test indicating TB infection.
Has a normal chest X-ray and negative sputum test.	May have an abnormal chest X-ray or positive sputum smear or culture.
Has TB bacteria in his/her body that are alive but inactive.	Has active TB bacteria in his/her body.
Does not feel sick.	Usually feels sick and may have symptoms such as coughing, fever and weight loss.
Cannot spread TB bacteria to others.	May spread TB bacteria to others.
Needs treatment for latent TB infection to prevent TB disease; however, if exposed and infected by a person with multidrug-resistant TB (MDR TB) or extensively drug-resistant TB (XDR TB), preventive treatment may not be an option.	Needs treatment to treat active TB disease.

Figure 4-2 *The difference between latent TB infection and active TB disease.*

The TST or a TB blood test is generally recommended for employees who are at risk because of being near people who may have TB, such as those employed in the workplaces listed earlier. Here are some special considerations for TB testing:

- The TB skin test is preferred over TB blood tests for children younger than 5 due to limited data on effectiveness.

- Some people with LTBI have a negative TST reaction when tested years after an infection. This occurs because the initial TST may stimulate (boost) their ability to react. Positive reactions to subsequent TSTs could be misinterpreted as indicating a recent infection.

- Someone who has another disease or illness is more likely to develop TB disease after an exposure and infection. Testing is even more important for someone with a compromised immune system because treatment may need to begin immediately.

- Two-step testing should be used for initial baseline M. tuberculosis testing of those who will be given a TST periodically such as health care workers and nursing care residents **(Table 4-1)**. This testing procedure helps to eliminate any confusion over whether an employee was infected previously or at the work site.

A positive skin test or blood test means an infection occurred, but these tests cannot distinguish between TB infection and TB disease. A chest X-ray and a sample of phlegm coughed up from the lungs are often needed to determine whether an infected person has TB disease. People found to have TB disease must be given treatment that involves administration of antibiotics over a 6-12-month period. The treatment is provided to employees by the employer if the TB infection is found to be work related.

Prevention of TB Infection

Although it is impossible to eliminate all risk of infection from TB in the workplace, the risk can be reduced. The 2005 CDC guidelines for preventing the transmission of TB in health care facilities recommend a 3-tiered hierarchy of infection controls to reduce TB transmission. They are:

- **Administrative controls** to reduce the risk of exposure through an effective infection control program

- **Environmental controls** to prevent the spread and reduce the concentration of droplet nuclei

- **Respiratory protection controls** to further reduce the risk of exposure in special areas and special circumstances.

Administrative controls are considered most important of the three infection control measures. Administrative controls include:

- Assigning responsibility for TB infection control (TBIC).

Table 4-1 **The 2-Step Test**

TST Result	Action
No previous test	Do 2-step test
First test positive	Consider TB infected
First test negative	Retest 1-3 weeks after first TST result was read
Second test positive	Consider TB infected
Second test negative	Consider not infected

- Working with the health department to conduct TB risk assessments and develop a written TBIC plan, including airborne infection isolation precautions.

- Ensuring timely lab processing and reporting.

- Implementing effective work practices for managing TB patients (e.g., using airborne infection isolation for TB patients).

- Testing and evaluating health care workers at risk for TB or for exposure to M. tuberculosis.

- Training health care workers about TB infection control.

- Ensuring proper cleaning of equipment.

- Using appropriate signage advising cough etiquette and respiratory hygiene.

After administrative controls, the second line of defense in a TB infection control program is environmental controls. They work to:

- Control the source of infection.

- Dilute and remove contaminated air.

- Control airflow (clean air to less-clean air).

Environmental controls remove or inactivate M. tuberculosis and consist of local exhaust ventilation, general ventilation and air-cleaning methods such as high-efficiency particulate air (HEPA) filtration and ultraviolet germicidal irradiation (UVGI).

The third level in the infection control hierarchy is respiratory protection controls. Respiratory protection should be used in settings where administrative and environmental controls will not prevent the inhalation of infectious droplet nuclei. Respiratory controls include:

- Implementing a respiratory protection program.

- Annual training of health care workers in respiratory protection.

- Initial and annual fit testing of health care workers' respiratory protection **(Figure 4-3).**

- Training patients in respiratory hygiene (see the section "Prevention of Flu Infection").

TB Exposure and Recordkeeping

Like an exposure to a bloodborne pathogen, an exposure to a known TB source should be reported to your employer. Similarly, you have a right to know if you have been exposed. After an exposure, you may be tested for TB, and if you are infected, your employer will make arrangements for appropriate treatment.

Employers must maintain records of employee exposure to TB, TST or TB blood test results and medical examinations. In addition, active TB disease must be reported to public health officials. States vary in their reporting requirements. The OSHA Form 300 log must

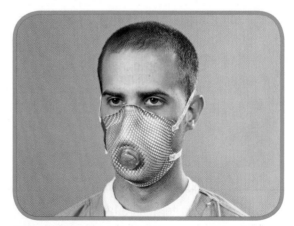

Figure 4-3 *A high-efficiency particulate air (HEPA) mask is used to prevent the spread of TB.*

be used to record both TB infections and TB disease unless there is clear documentation the exposure and subsequent infection or disease occurred outside a work setting.

Treatment of TB

TB infections can be treated, although sometimes the person is not treated if there is little risk of the disease resulting. Factors that influence this decision include the person's age, overall health, lifestyle and occupation.

TB disease can be cured by a combination of several different antibiotics generally taken for 6-12 months. The drugs must be taken exactly as prescribed. This is because many bacteria must be killed. Taking several medications will do a better job of killing all of the bacteria and preventing them from becoming resistant to the medicines. TB bacteria die very slowly. Because it takes at least 6 months for the medicine to kill all the TB bacteria, a person must continue to take the medicine until all the TB bacteria are dead, even though he or she may feel better and have no more symptoms of active TB disease.

Influenza

Influenza, or flu, is caused by a virus that infects the respiratory tract (nose, throat, lungs). Most people who get the flu will not need the medical care of antiviral drugs, and will recover in less than 2 weeks. Some people are likely to get flu complications that can result in being hospitalized and occasionally result in death. Pneumonia, bronchitis, and sinus and ear infections are examples of flu-related complications. The flu can make chronic health problems such as congestive heart failure worse.

Groups of people more likely to develop flu-related complications once infected with the flu include children younger than 5 (especially children younger than 2), adults 65 and older

(continues on page 45)

 ## Learning Checkpoint 1

1. True or False: Infection with an airborne pathogen is more likely for people with certain medical conditions.

2. True or False: The symptoms of TB disease include fever, night sweats and general weakness.

3. True or False: The CDC advises all work sites to have anti-TB respirators available for employees who choose to use them.

4. Employees in what work settings may face a greater risk of exposure to TB?
   (Check all that apply.)

   _____ a. Health care facilities   _____ e. Restaurants

   _____ b. Homeless shelters   _____ f. Correctional facilities

   _____ c. Public schools   _____ g. Drug treatment centers

   _____ d. Long-term care facilities   _____ h. Recreational centers open to the public

5. True or False: As with HCV and HIV, there is no cure for TB disease.

(continued from page 44)

and pregnant women. People with certain medical conditions are more likely to get flu-related complications. These medical conditions include: asthma, chronic lung disease (e.g., chronic obstructive pulmonary disease (COPD), heart disease (e.g., coronary artery disease), blood disorders (e.g., sickle cell disease), endocrine disorders (e.g., diabetes mellitus), kidney or liver disorders and people with a weakened immune system due to disease or medication (e.g., people with cancer or HIV/AIDS).

How Is Influenza Spread?

People with flu can spread it to others up to 6 feet away via airborne transmission. Most experts think the flu viruses are spread mainly by droplets made when people with flu cough, sneeze or talk. These droplets can land in the mouths or noses of nearby people or be inhaled into the lungs. A typical secondary method of transmission involves a person touching a surface or object that has flu virus on it and then touching their own nose or mouth.

The flu is very contagious. Most healthy adults may be able to infect others beginning 1 day before symptoms develop and up to 5-7 days after becoming sick. Children may pass the virus for longer than 7 days. Symptoms start 1-4 days after the virus enters the body.

Symptoms of the Flu

Symptoms of the flu may include the following:

- Cough
- Runny or stuffy nose
- Thick mucus
- Muscle pain
- Stiffness
- Fatigue
- Headache
- Sore throat
- Shaking, chills
- Fever
- Dehydration
- Difficulty breathing

It is rare for the flu to cause vomiting. If you have vomiting as a symptom, you probably do not have the flu, but you might have gastroenteritis instead. Some people can be infected with the flu virus but have no symptoms. During this time, those people may still spread the virus to others.

Prevention of Flu Infection

There are 4 ways to avoid getting the flu.

1. **Hand hygiene.** Scrupulous hand washing is one of the best ways to prevent infection. **Lesson 3** gives guidelines for hand washing and the use of alcohol-based hand rub. You should wash your hands in all of the following situations:

- Before preparing or eating food
- After going to the bathroom
- After handling garbage
- After touching public items and surfaces
- After blowing your nose, coughing or sneezing
- Before and after tending a sick person
- Before and after treating a cut or wound
- After handling an animal or animal waste
- After changing diapers or cleaning up a child who has gone to the bathroom
- Before and after using medical exam gloves

2. **Respiratory hygiene.** Good respiratory hygiene includes the following behaviors:

- Cover your nose and mouth with a tissue when coughing or sneezing.

- If you do not have a tissue, cough into your upper sleeve instead of your hand.

- Dispose of tissues in the nearest waste receptacle and immediately wash your hands.

- Avoid touching your eyes, nose and mouth.

- Wear a surgical mask if you are sick or if you are around sick people.

3. **Social distancing.** To practice social distancing, you should:

- Avoid crowded settings.

- Make the time short if you have to be in a crowd.

- Stay away from people who are sick.

- Keep at least 6 feet away from any sick person with whom you must come in contact.

- Stay at home if you are sick.

- Keep your children at home if they are sick.

4. **Immunization.** A flu shot will protect you from seasonal flu. The CDC recommends that everyone 6 months and older get a yearly flu vaccine. It takes about 2 weeks after vaccination for the body to develop an immune response.

Taking Care of Those Infected with Flu

There is no cure for the flu. However, when you or someone in your family gets sick with the flu, you can take certain measures. To prevent exposing others and making symptoms worse,

the infected person should stay home. He or she should also:

- Get plenty of rest.

- Drink lots of fluids.

- Avoid alcohol and tobacco.

- Take medications to relieve flu symptoms.

- Call a medical professional if a high fever develops.

- Consider wearing a surgical mask around others.

Only one person should be the caregiver for an infected person. The caregiver should do the following:

- Avoid mingling personal items such as computers, pens, clothes, towels, sheets, blankets, food and eating utensils.

- Disinfect door knobs, switches, handles, toys and other surfaces touched around the home or workplace.

- Wash hands frequently.

- Wear disposable gloves when in contact with body fluids.

Everyone's dishes and clothes can be washed together, but detergent and very hot water should be used. Hands should be washed after dirty laundry is handled.

Types of Flu

There are many types of flu. Two common types are seasonal influenza and avian influenza (bird flu).

Seasonal flu is the respiratory illness that occurs every year, usually in the fall and winter. In the United States, influenza season usually begins in October and can last until May. Everyone gets seasonal flu at some point in their lives, and most have some immunity. A vaccine can provide additional immunity. Every region in the world has seasonal flu. However, different regions have different seasons and viruses. Most people recover from seasonal flu, but many people die each year from seasonal flu infection. The number varies depending on the predominant flu virus. According to the CDC, the number of deaths over the past 31 years ranges from 3,000-49,000.[2]

Bird flu infects wild birds and domestic poultry. The degree of pathogenicity varies. Birds naturally carry low-pathogenic flu virus and have mild or no symptoms. But a low-pathogenic virus can mutate and become highly pathogenic. When this happens, it spreads rapidly among birds, and the death rate is high. Bird flu has jumped species to infect humans when they have close contact with birds or their feces or with intermediate hosts like pigs **(Figure 4-4)**. Though rare, humans have also caught bird flu from close contact with other infected humans.

[2](http://www.cdc.gov/flu/about/disease/us_flu-related_deaths.htm Accessed 9/22/11)

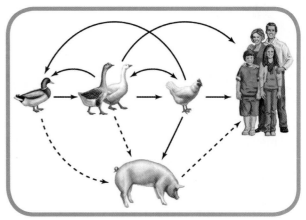

Figure 4-4 *How bird flu spreads.*

Epidemics and Pandemics

An **epidemic** is an outbreak of a disease in a community or region. A **pandemic** is an epidemic that spreads beyond a community or region throughout the world. Currently, there is no flu pandemic. However, the 2009 H1N1 virus caused the first global pandemic in more than 40 years and resulted in illness, hospitalizations and death. On August 10, 2010, a committee of the World Health Organization (WHO) declared an end to the H1N1 pandemic globally. Still, H1N1 viruses will likely continue to spread for years to come, like a regular seasonal influenza.

Learning Checkpoint 2

1. True or False: Good respiratory hygiene includes coughing into your hand when you do not have a tissue.

2. True or False: A flu shot will protect you from seasonal flu.

3. Check off which symptoms may be present with flu:

   _____ a. Stiffness   _____ d. Sore throat

   _____ b. Shaking chills   _____ e. Abdominal pain

   _____ c. Vomiting   _____ f. Difficulty breathing

4. True or False: When taking care of a family member infected with the flu virus, you should wash that person's dishes and laundry separately to avoid infecting other family members.

Sample Hepatitis B Vaccine Declination Form

I understand that due to my occupational exposure to blood or other potentially infectious materials I may be at risk of acquiring hepatitis B virus (HBV) infection. I have been given the opportunity to be vaccinated with hepatitis B vaccine, at no charge to myself. However, I decline hepatitis B vaccination at this time. I understand that by declining this vaccine, I continue to be at risk of acquiring hepatitis B, a serious disease. If in the future I continue to have occupational exposure to blood or other potentially infectious materials and I want to be vaccinated with hepatitis B vaccine, I can receive the vaccination series at no charge to me.

Employee: _____

Signature: _____   Date: _____

Supervisor: _____

Signature: _____   Date:_____

Sample Exposure Incident Report Form

Please read this form and the instructions thoroughly before filling out the form. Immediate supervisor should complete this form promptly with employee input. Please print clearly and forward to the Risk Manager.

1. _____
   Employee

2. _____
   Immediate Supervisor

3. _____
   Date of Incident

4. _____
   Time

5. _____
   Incident Location and Case Number (if applicable)

6. Describe the incident fully (route of exposure, circumstances; describe type of controls in place at time of incident including engineering controls and personal protective equipment worn; identify unsafe conditions and/or actions; relevant police reports).

   _____

   _____

   _____

7. Describe employee's injury (part of the body/type of injury).

   _____

   _____

8. Describe first aid/medical treatment (when and by whom).

   _____

   _____

9. When was the incident reported? _____

   To whom? _____

   If not immediately reported, why? _____

10. List names of witnesses. _____

_____

_____

11. Is the source individual known? Yes _____ No _____

If yes, please provide name/address so that a consent for blood testing can be obtained.

Name: _____

Address: _____

DID THE SOURCE CONSENT TO BLOOD DRAW AND TESTING?

Yes _____ No _____

12. What corrective action was taken or is planned to prevent similar incidents from occurring in the future?

_____

_____

_____

13. Referral to medical evaluator? Yes _____ No _____ Date: _____

If no, explain: _____

NAME OF INVESTIGATOR: _____

TITLE: _____

DATE: _____

(Adapted from The Oregon Occupational Safety & Health Division)

Sample Sharps Injury Log
(Example 1)

The following information, if known or reasonably available, must be documented within 14 working days of the date on which each exposure incident was reported.

1. Date and time of the exposure incident: _____

2. Date of exposure incident report:_____ Report written by: _____

3. Type and brand of sharp involved: _____

4. Description of exposure incident: _____
   - Job classification of exposed employee: _____
   - Department or work area where the incident occurred: _____
   - Procedure being performed by the exposed employee at the time of the incident:
     _____
   - How the incident occurred: _____
   - Bodypart(s) involved: _____
   - Did the device involved have engineered sharps injury protection? Yes_____ No_____
   - Was engineered sharps injury protection on the sharp involved? Yes_____ No_____

   If yes:

   A. Was the protective mechanism activated at the time of the exposure incident?
      Yes_____ No_____

   B. Did the injury occur before, during, or after the mechanism was activated?

   If no:

   A. Does the injured employee believe that a protective mechanism could have prevented the injury?
      Yes_____ No_____

   Comments: _____
   _____

   - Does the exposed employee believe that any controls (e.g., engineering, administrative or work practice) could have prevented the injury? Yes_____ No_____

   Employee's opinion: _____
   _____

5. Comments on the exposure incident (e.g., additional relevant factors involved):
   _____
   _____

6. Employee interview summary: _____

7. Picture(s) of the sharp(s) involved (please attach if available).

(Adapted from CAL/OSHA Exposure Control Plan for Bloodborne Pathogens)

Sample Sharps Injury Log
(Example 2)

Establishment/facility name:_____ Year:_____

Date	Case report number	Type of device (e.g., syringe, suture, needle)	Brand name and name of device	Work area where injury occured (e.g., Geriatrics, Lab)	Brief description of how the incident occured (i.e., procedure being performed [disposal, injection, etc.]), body part injured

Retain for 5 years

Sample Exposure Control Plan

Facility name: _____

Date of preparation: _____

We, the management staff of ___(name of organization)___, are committed to the prevention of incidents or happenings that result in employee injury and illness and to compliance with the OSHA Bloodborne Pathogens Standard. Through this written Exposure Control Plan, we share assigned responsibility and hereby adopt this Exposure Control Plan as an element of the ___(name of organization)___ Safety and Health Program.

A. Purpose

   The purposes of this Exposure Control Plan:

   1. To eliminate or minimize employee occupational exposure to blood or other body fluids.

   2. To identify employees occupationally exposed to blood or other potentially infectious materials (OPIM) in the performance of their regular job duties.

   3. To provide employees exposed to blood and OPIM information and training. A copy of this plan is available to all employees during the work shift at __(location)__.

   4. To comply with OSHA Bloodborne Pathogens Standard.

B. Exposure determination

   (Name of organization) has performed an exposure determination for all common job classifications that may be expected to incur occupational exposures to blood or other potentially infectious materials. This exposure determination is made without regard to use of PPE. The following job classifications may be expected to incur occupational exposures to blood or other potentially infectious materials:

   (List job classifications)

   _____

   _____

   The following is a list of job classifications in which some employees may have occupational exposures to blood or OPIM:

   Job classification   Task or procedure

   _____   _____

   _____   _____

   _____   _____

Sample Forms

C. Compliance methods

1. Universal precautions

This organization embraces "universal precautions," which is a method of infection control that requires the employer and employee to assume that all human blood and human body fluids are infected with bloodborne pathogens. Where it is difficult or impossible to identify body fluids, all are to be considered potentially infectious.

2. Engineering controls and work practices

The following engineering and work practice controls will be used by all employees to eliminate or minimize occupational exposures at this facility:

(List all controls necessary and practical to protect employees.)

Engineering controls

a. Contaminated disposable sharps will be disposed of…

b. _____

c. _____

(List all procedures used or required to protect employees.)

Work practice controls

a. Wash hands with soap and water after…

_____

b. Flush eyes and mucous membranes immediately after…

_____

c. Eating, drinking and etc. not allowed in…

_____

3. Personal protective equipment (PPE)

The following PPE will be provided at no cost to employees:

(List required PPE and when used.)

a. Body protection: (List items and when used.)

_____

_____

b. Gloves and masks: (Indicate when and where used.)

_____

_____

c. Eye protection: (List tasks requiring eye protection.)

_____

_____

d. Special PPE:

_____

_____

The (job title) is responsible for ensuring and issuing appropriate, readily accessible PPE, without cost, to employees. Hypoallergenic gloves, glove liners, powderless gloves or similar alternatives shall be readily accessible to employees who are allergic to the gloves normally provided.

All PPE will be removed prior to leaving the work area.

All PPE will be cleaned, laundered and disposed of by the employer at no cost to the employee. PPE, when removed, will be placed in the (designated area) for storage, washing, decontamination and disposal.

4. Housekeeping

This facility will be cleaned and decontaminated according to the following schedule:

Area	Schedule	Cleaner

5. Contaminated laundry

(List organization's procedures.)

Contaminated laundry will be cleaned at _(location)_ .

6. Regulated waste

The following procedures will be followed:

(List organization's procedures.)

Sample Forms

7. Hepatitis B vaccine and post-exposure evaluation and follow-up

Hepatitis B vaccination

(Organization's name) will offer the hepatitis B vaccine and vaccination series at no cost to exposed employees. The company will offer post-exposure follow-up at no cost to employees.

The (job title) is in charge of the hepatitis B vaccination program.

(List organization's procedures.)

The (list person or persons) will ensure that all medical evaluations and procedures, including the hepatitis B vaccine and vaccination series and post-exposure follow-up, including prophylaxis, are made available at no charge to the employee at a reasonable place and time, and performed or supervised by a licensed health care professional according to the recommendations of the CDC.

Post-exposure evaluation and follow-up

When an employee has an exposure incident, it will be reported to (job title).

(List organization's procedures.)

Following a reported exposure incident, the exposed employee will immediately receive a confidential medical evaluation including the following elements:

(List medical evaluation elements.)

All employees who incur an exposure incident will be offered post-exposure evaluation and follow-up in accordance with the standard. All post-exposure follow-ups will be performed by (clinic, physician, or department).

Information provided to the health care professional

The (job title) will ensure that the health care professional responsible for the employee's hepatitis B vaccination receives the following:

(List information required.)

Health care professional's written opinion

The (job title) will obtain and provide the employee with a copy of the evaluating health care professional's written opinion within 15 days of the completion of the evaluation.

The health care professional's written opinion for HBV vaccination will be limited to whether HBV is indicated for and has been received by the employee.

The health care professional's written opinion for post-exposure follow-up will be limited to the following information:

(List information.)

8. Labels and signs

The (job title) will ensure biohazard labels are on each container of regulated waste.

(List items that require labeling.)

9. Information and training

The (job title) will ensure that employees are trained prior to initial assignment to tasks in which occupational exposure may occur and that training shall be repeated within 12 months. The training program will be tailored to the education level and language of the employees and will be offered during the normal work shift. The training will be interactive and will contain the following information:

(List information required.)

Additional training will be given to employees when changes of tasks or procedures affect employees' occupational exposure.

10. Recordkeeping

The (job title) is responsible for maintaining medical records as indicated below. These records will be kept (location).

11. Training records

The (job title) is responsible for maintaining the following records. These records will be kept at (location). (List records to be kept.)

Employee records will be made available to the employee.

D.   Evaluation and review

(This section recommended)

The (job title or titles) is/are responsible for reviewing this program and its effectiveness (annually or as needed) and for updating it as needed.

Adopted (date), by (highest management official).

(Adapted from the Oregon Occupational Safety & Health Division, based on the OSHA Bloodborne Pathogens Standard.)

Sample Forms

Sample Bloodborne Pathogens Training Log

Date of Training: _____

Name of Instructor: _____

Attach:

- Paragraph stating the instructor's qualifications to teach this course

- Photocopy of the "Table of Contents" from the student's NSC Bloodborne & Airborne Pathogens text

Name	Job Classification	Received or told where to review a copy of the Bloodborne Pathogens Standard (check)	Received or told where to review a copy of the Exposure Control Plan (check)

Retain for 3 years.

Index